Sunset
Maui
TRAVEL GUIDE

By the Editors of
Sunset Books and Sunset Magazine

LANE PUBLISHING CO. • Menlo Park, California

Mahalo...

The editors of Sunset Books are grateful to all of the people and organizations who contributed to this publication. We particularly appreciate the help we received from the Maui Visitors Bureau, Maui Chamber of Commerce, Kaanapali Beach Operators Association, Lahaina Restoration Foundation, Lynn Britton, Andy and Janey Clark, Donna Del Rio, Mary Gresham, and Tom Morrow.

For their editorial assistance, a special thanks to Marianne Lipanovich and Teri Ann Johnson.

Hours, admission fees, prices, telephone numbers, and highway designations in this book are accurate as of the time this edition went to press.

Sunset Books
    Editor: David E. Clark
    Managing Editor: Elizabeth L. Hogan

First printing May 1987

Bird of paradise

Plumeria

Ginger

BOOK EDITOR
BARBARA J. BRAASCH

COORDINATING EDITOR
SUZANNE N. MATHISON

DESIGN
JOANN MASAOKA

MAPS
**JOHN PARSONS,
EUREKA CARTOGRAPHY**

ILLUSTRATIONS
CHAD KUBO

HAWAII CONSULTANTS,
SUNSET MAGAZINE
**NANCY BANNICK
JEFF PHILLIPS**

Cover: A tranquil setting for snorkelers, sailors, and sunlovers, famed Kapalua Beach attracts visitors and *kama'ainas* (natives) to Maui's northwest coast. Photographed by Marie Mainz.

Photographers

Ken Bates: 62 all. **Chris Fesler:** 15 left, 44 top. **David Franzen:** 2 bottom, 37, 38 all. **Mark E. Gibson:** 10 top, 16 bottom, 25 bottom. **Jeff Gnass:** 9, 36. **Cliff Hollenbeck:** 16 top, 17, 46, 54 left. **Dave G. Houser:** 32, 45, 51, 59, 61. **Greg Kaufman:** 18. **Rene Klein:** 24. **Greg Lawson:** 10 bottom. **Marie Mainz:** 1. **David Muench:** 31. **Suzanne Murphy:** 8, 25 top. **Papillon Helicopters/John Henry:** 43. **Douglas Peebles:** 26, 52. **Norman Plate:** 23. **Allan Seiden:** 53, 60. **Elliott Varner Smith:** 44 bottom. **Ted Streshinsky:** 7. **Tom Tracy:** 2 center. **Darrow Watt:** 2 top. **R. Wenkam:** 15 right, 35, 54 right.

Contents

Special Features

The Valley Isle

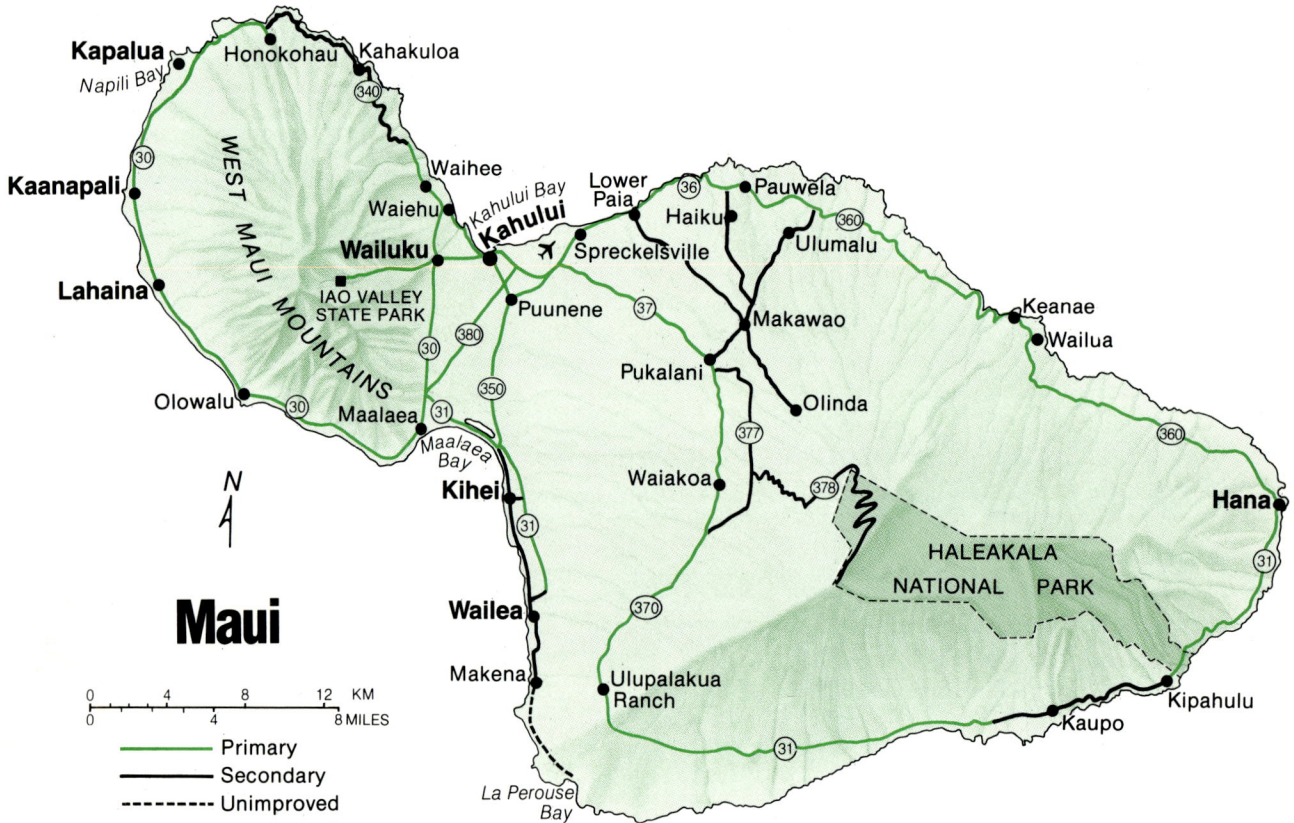

Maui map with the following labeled locations and features:

Towns and places: Kapalua, Napili Bay, Honokohau, Kahakuloa, Kaanapali, Waihee, Waiehu, Lower Paia, Pauwela, Lahaina, Wailuku, Kahului, Kahului Bay, Haiku, Ulumalu, IAO VALLEY STATE PARK, Spreckelsville, Puunene, Makawao, Keanae, Wailua, Olowalu, Maalaea, Pukalani, Olinda, Maalaea Bay, Kihei, Waiakoa, Hana, Wailea, Makena, Ulupalakua Ranch, HALEAKALA NATIONAL PARK, La Perouse Bay, Kaupo, Kipahulu

Mountains: WEST MAUI MOUNTAINS

Route numbers: 340, 30, 36, 360, 37, 380, 350, 31, 377, 378, 370

Maui

Scale: 0 4 8 12 KM / 0 4 8 MILES

Legend:
— Primary
— Secondary
----- Unimproved

The minute you get off the plane at Kahului Airport, Maui introduces itself to you through one of its more subtle specialties—breezes, from sea and valley, that somehow are *Maui* breezes, different in certain indefinable ways from those of any other place. Varying from gentle morning breezes to brisk afternoon tradewinds, they frequently carry the delicate fragrances of the tropics. Chances are that you will notice and appreciate them throughout your stay—and remember them always.

Maui No Ka Oi

Hospitable Maui has a slogan, *Maui No Ka Oi,* "Maui is the best." Certainly few destinations rival the island's warm, friendly atmosphere, and it is a place of almost endless discovery. An increasing number of visitors succumb to its charm, returning year after year—with their friends.

Hawaii's second largest island (729 square miles) offers superb beaches, fine golf and tennis facilities, and a world of family activity. There is plenty for hikers, bikers, joggers, horseback riders, garden enthusiasts, whale watchers, shoppers, bird lovers, gourmets, or just plain tired-out visitors wanting to relax and "unwind."

Sightseeing ranges from the heights of Haleakala to the scenic and invigorating upcountry ranchlands to the historic former whaling town of Lahaina—attractions so different from one another that the visitor may wonder "Can this be the same island?"

Until the late 1960s, Maui was known primarily for its agriculture, despite the fact that Kaanapali, on the west Maui coast, was already beginning to develop into the island's first major resort area. In recent years several other resort areas have been developed, increasing tourism dramatically. Agriculture, though still strong, has declined to some extent; many island residents (permanent population numbers 70,000) whose

4

forebears worked in the pineapple and cane fields now find employment in resorts, restaurants, and retail stores.

Island Geography

Maui began existence as two separate land masses. Centuries of erosion from their slopes formed the isthmus that joins them today. From that isthmus Maui gained its famed nickname, the "Valley Isle." Cane fields now blanket the irrigated plain between the mountains, and sugarcane and pineapple cover the foothills. And spread out from where the plain meets the ocean to the north are Maui's two largest towns, Wailuku and Kahului.

On the 5,788-foot summit of the West Maui Mountains, Puu Kukui, more than 400 inches of rain falls annually, making it second to Kauai's Waialeale as Hawaii's rainiest peak.

On the other side of the isthmus, the great mass of the dormant volcano Haleakala rises to 10,023 feet. Its cool, grassy slopes provide grazing for cattle and other livestock, and vegetables and flowers are grown here for commercial markets.

At the foot of Haleakala's eastern slope, standing in contrast to the changing picture throughout most of Maui, is gentle old Hana—where an always-easy pace combines with geographical remoteness to make the area seem almost like an island in itself.

How's the Weather?

With almost perfect weather, Maui beckons year-round. Though it lies in the tropics, fresh trade winds from the east and northeast prevail most of the year, keeping the air pleasantly balmy. In lowland areas, such as beaches, temperatures range from an average low of 65° to an average high of 80° in winter, and from 73° to 88° in summer. Atop Haleakala, the temperature occasionally drops into the 20s, and in the upcountry sections the range is from the low 50s to the low 70s. The water temperature varies even less—75° to 82°.

Sometimes the trades break down and a spell of *kona* (a leeward wind) weather sets in, with southwesterly breezes and high humidity. In summer and early autumn, a kona wind is synonymous with sticky weather; in winter it brings a few storms (gales and torrential rains) but also some of the island's clearest days.

Winter trades can get blustery and drop frequent showers even on the driest leeward areas. In spring and summer, showers are few and come mostly at night, drifting down from the mountain peaks. The surprise of island weather is that a year's rain may amount to more than 100 inches in one place and less than 20 in another just a few miles away.

There's an old saying in the islands that "the winter of the tropics is the night." Here the temperature difference is greater between day and night than between the coldest and warmest time of the year.

What to Wear

Lightweight clothing is the rule throughout the year. Around resorts and for touring, women wear casual attire (short *mu'umu'us,* shorts, or pants); men wear sport shirts with shorts or slacks. Bring a scarf or hat to protect hair from island breezes.

Informal clothes are also suitable in the evening; a few elegant restaurants do require men to wear a coat and tie. A sweater or lightweight jacket is often welcome on a cool evening or in an air-conditioned restaurant. A fold-up umbrella is useful during occasional rainy periods (a raincoat is usually too warm); take lightweight rain gear, though, if you plan to do much hiking or camping.

Shopping~Almost a Sport

For anyone who enjoys shopping, Maui offers a variety of stores, boutiques, and art galleries. Even those who generally don't indulge may find some pleasant surprises, such as the wide variety of seashells and coral available in specialty stores and souvenir shops.

When you're grocery shopping, make it a point to try Maui Potato Chips (made in Kahului). Maui is also the home of the sweet Kula onion; once you've tried them, you're sure to want to take a bag back home.

Most areas boast one or more large shopping centers. *Kahului:* Kaahumanu Center, Kahului Shopping Center, Maui Mall; *Lahaina:* Lahaina Market Place, Lahaina Shopping Center, Mariner's Alley, Wharf Shopping Complex, Dickenson Square, The Cannery; *Kaanapali:* Whalers Village; *Kihei:* Azeka Place, Kihei Town Center, Rainbow Mall; *Wailea:* Wailea Shopping Village; *Pukalani:* Pukalani Terrace Center.

Resort hotels have some excellent shops, as do several of the small towns. Makawao, especially, is an off-the-beaten-path shopping experience.

Scrimshaw shops in Lahaina offer a wide variety of old and new pieces, ranging from a few dollars to collector's item prices. This meticulous art—the carving or engraving of ivory, bone, and whales' teeth—goes back hundreds of years. Among the finest scrimshanders were the sailors who manned the whaling ships; many a whale's tooth took shape under the skilled hands of these seafarers who found scrimshaw to be a good way to pass the often lonesome weeks and months at sea. But since the Endangered Species Act of 1973 prohibited importation of whale products into the United States, scrimshanders turned to other media, especially fossil ivory.

Planning Your Trip

Maui lies about 2,400 miles southwest of California. By air, the trip takes approximately 5 hours from West Coast cities, 9 hours from Chicago, and 11 hours from New York. Hawaiian Standard Time is 2 hours ahead of Pacific. The area code for all of Hawaii is 808.

Getting to Maui

You'll have your choice of airlines. Most have been flying to the islands for many years. Among the largest and best known are American, CP Air, Continental, Delta, Hawaiian, Northwest Orient, TWA, United, and Western. Several of these airlines offer direct service to Kahului from the mainland (with a stop in Honolulu); a few provide nonstop flights.

Passengers booked on foreign airlines cannot fly solely between two U.S. cities (San Francisco and Honolulu, for example), but they are permitted a stopover in Hawaii en route to or from a foreign destination.

Interisland flights. Frequent interisland flights connect all major island airports and serve most smaller ones at least once a day. Aloha Airlines, Hawaiian Airlines, and Mid Pacific Airlines serve the islands of Maui, Oahu, Kauai, and Hawaii.

Air Molokai-Tropic and Reeves airlines connect Maui, Molokai, and Lanai with Honolulu. Princeville Airways makes daily round trips to Honolulu, Kauai, Maui, and Hawaii.

Airports. Major air carriers fly into Kahului Airport, Maui's largest. Commuter planes also use the smaller Kapalua-West Maui airport; Princeville has daily flights between Kahului and the Hana airport.

Getting Around

A cursory glance at a map might lead you to believe that a circle trip around the island is possible. It's not advisable, though, since certain stretches of road on the northern and southeastern extremities of the island are unimproved and can be dangerous, particularly during and after heavy rains.

From Kahului, it's about 40 miles to the top of Haleakala and about 50 miles to Hana; these trips take longer than the distances indicate, though, because part of the route is over narrow, winding roads.

Most of Maui's highways are excellent; auto exploring or simply getting from one place to another is

pleasant and relatively easy—except for early morning and late afternoon commute hours.

Car rental. Before you rent a vehicle in Maui, check the various rates and special packages that are offered; there are many from which to choose. It's a good idea to make auto reservations in advance. Because many roads are narrow by mainland standards, drivers generally prefer compact cars to larger models.

In our limited space it is impossible to list every car rental agency on Maui; you'll find all the nationwide companies (Avis, Budget, Dollar, Hertz, National, and Thrifty). In addition, the following agencies rent cars on all the major islands: Alamo, American, Island Shores, Odyssey, Robert's, Tropical, and United. If you choose to shop around after you arrive, you'll find many local rental agencies.

Bus and shuttle service. Grayline-Maui and Roberts offer shuttle service (reservations only) between the Kahului Airport and major resort areas. Taxi and limo service is also available, but costly because of the distances involved.

Shoreline buses operate throughout the day between Kahului and Wailuku and West Maui with stops at hotels along the route. Kaanapali Trolley (free) roams the spread-out resort area of Kaanapali. The Lahaina Kaanapali & Pacific Railroad (see page 17) runs for 6 miles between Kaanapali and Lahaina stations.

Where to Stay

Most Maui vacationers head for one of three regional bases: Lahaina and Kaanapali on the west coast, Napili Bay and Kapalua on the northwest coast, or the southwest oceanfront areas from Kihei south to Wailea and Makena. The Kahului-Wailuku area in northcentral Maui makes a good base for visitors on business; it is also a convenient hub for those interested primarily in sightseeing. Our listing of accommodations starts on page 56.

West Maui. The resort region extends north from Lahaina, with its colorful Pioneer Inn, to the luxurious Kapalua Bay Hotel and condominium villas. Kaanapali Beach Resort has six deluxe hotels, all on sandy swimming beaches. Numerous condominiums, apartment hotels, apartments, and cottages also line the coast all the way north to Napili Bay. Wherever you stay in west Maui, you will be only a few minutes away from four

Cowboys and canoes, festivals and feasts, pageants and parades all combine in the colorful kaleidoscope of special events that Maui offers to visitors. Flower and craft shows, rodeos, athletic competitions, and religious ceremonies abound.

The Maui Visitors Bureau (172 Alamaha St., Suite 100, Kahului, HI 96732) and hotel activities desks provide information on events of interest.

January
Narcissus Festival for Chinese New Year

February
Cherry Blossom Festival

March
Maui Marathon, Kahului to Kaanapali
Prince Kuhio Day

April
Buddha Day

May
Hal "Aku" Lewis Golf and Tennis Tournaments, Wailea
Lei Day
Valley Isle Triathlon, Wailea

Annual Events & Festivities

Annual canoe races

June
King Kamehameha Day
Upcountry Fun Fair, Makawao

July
Canoe races, Hookipa State Park
4th of July Rodeo, Makawao
Yacht Club races, Lahaina

August
Run to the Sun, Kahului to Haleakala

September
Aloha Week festivities
Windsurf for the Whales, Wailea

October
Maui County Fair, Kahului

November
Hui Noeau Christmas Craft Fair, Makawao
Isuzu International Golf Championship, Kapalua
Na Mele O Maui festival, Kaanapali/ Lahaina

December
Hawaii International Film Festival, Kaanapali

18-hole golf courses—two at Kaanapali and two at Kapalua (see page 50).

Southwest Coast. The leeward side of Haleakala has undergone continual development, particularly since the mid-1970s. You'll still find some popular "traditional" places, such as the Maui Lu Resort, very much in business. But many new condominiums and apartments are strung out along the coast from Maalaea Bay through Kihei. Farther south, Wailea has two resort hotels and several nice condominium villages, plus two 18-hole golf courses (see page 51).

Past Wailea, at Makena, an 18-hole golf course and condominium complex has been joined by the Maui Prince Hotel.

Elsewhere on the island. Isolated by choice, "heavenly Hana" attracts visitors content to absorb the beauty of the island's windward side. Accommodations are limited to the prestigious Hotel Hana Maui, a coastside condominium complex, a small inn, and scattered rental houses. You'll also find a choice of accommodations at Kula, up on Haleakala's slopes.

What to Do

Maui has something for everyone. In the recreation guide, beginning on page 42, you'll discover a variety of outdoor activities. Tour companies offer a wide choice of sightseeing options, including trips to Hana, Lahaina, Iao Valley, and upcountry to Haleakala. You can see the island from the air by small plane or helicopter or get out on the water on a boat cruise. Sailing, deep-sea fishing, whale watching (winter months only), or a voyage to the best snorkeling waters are among the possibilities. Other special activities include horseback riding, cycling down Haleakala, hiking, and camping in a crater. The Valley Isle boasts some of the country's finest golf courses and best tennis facilities.

Dining & Entertainment

Maui's profusion of restaurants cover the gamut from budget-priced fast food to the finest and most expensive cuisine. Many are right on the ocean shore, offering tables with a view. The lanai settings at some of the hotels make it difficult to determine whether you are dining indoors or out. A representative selection of restaurants—and cuisines—throughout the island starts on page 61. You'll make other happy discoveries during your stay.

There's plenty of music and entertainment to choose from, especially at the resort hotels. Late-night activity is particularly lively around Lahaina's bustling waterfront and at Kaanapali.

Kahului/Wailuku

Maui's business and commerce centers around Wailuku and Kahului, adjoining towns at the northern end of the isthmus separating the West Maui Mountains from Haleakala.

Wailuku, older of the two towns, is charmingly situated on the slopes of the West Maui Mountains at the mouth of Iao Valley. Narrow, hilly streets, wooden shops, tree-shaded residential lanes, and the handsome buildings in its historic district give the town a look of the past in spite of a growing number of modern office buildings. Wailuku is the seat of Maui County (which includes the islands of Lanai and Molokai). You can't miss seeing Kalana O Maui, the 9-story county office building that towers over its older neighbors in the government complex.

Kahului, 3 miles downhill alongside Kahului Bay, is Maui's deep-water port. Several hotels and three shopping centers face Kaahumanu Avenue, the main thoroughfare. Kahului Airport is just east of town.

A few minutes drive northwest of Wailuku is Waiehu Golf Course, a scenic and challenging 18-hole layout with an ocean setting. Just beyond is Waihee, a small plantation settlement. From here, the road winds through and around the West Maui Mountains (see page 19); many stretches are unimproved.

Three routes cross the isthmus from the island hub to Maalaea Bay at the south. From Wailuku, Honoapiilani Highway (Highway 30) skirts the West Maui

Mountains and leads to Lahaina, Kaanapali, and the other West Maui resort areas. Monkeypod-lined Puunene Avenue goes to Puunene Mill (headquarters of Hawaiian Commercial & Sugar Company), where it connects with Highway 350 to Kihei and Maui's southwest shore. Highway 380 runs southwest from Puunene to Highway 30, which then proceeds to Maalaea Bay and on up to Lahaina and points north.

Kahului~Port City

Kahului, Maui's port city, is rapidly expanding with new business and commercial developments. There are several excellent restaurants (see page 61).

Starting at the airport and continuing west through Kahului toward Wailuku, here are a few places of interest:

Kanaha Beach Park runs along the beach just above the airport. You can picnic here beneath large shade trees and enjoy a panoramic view across the water. To reach the park, turn off the airport road at the Department of Water Supply baseyard near the terminal, then turn right on Alahao Street.

Kanaha Pond, between the airport and Kahului, was an ancient royal fishpond. Now it's Hawaii's most important native and migratory waterfowl bird refuge, particularly for the Hawaiian stilt. Its low water levels also attract a variety of migratory shorebirds.

Kahului Harbor, Maui's deep-water port, has the state's first bulk sugar plant and acts as a fueling base for several hundred Japanese fishing boats each year. Adjacent Hoaloha Park is a pleasant picnic spot and resting place. American Hawaii Cruises often anchors in the bay, transferring passengers to shore for sightseeing trips.

Three shopping complexes, Kahului Shopping Center, Maui Mall, and Kaahumanu Center front a half-mile stretch of Kaahumanu Avenue. Kahului Shopping Center, oldest of the three, is gradually giving way to newer Maui Mall and Kaahumanu Center, but its well-worn benches in the cool shade of burgeoning old monkeypod trees are still a favorite gathering place for local residents. The three centers offer an assortment of shops, ranging from small boutiques and specialty stores to department stores and supermarkets. Here, too, are several restaurants, snack bars, and take-out counters featuring local foods. Special entertainment is staged frequently at all three centers.

Keeping old traditions alive,
tutu *(grandmother) shows* keikis *(children)*
how to plant a taro field.

A Maui landmark, Iao Needle juts up from verdant valley floor.
Iao Stream cascades in foreground.

Maui Community College, part of the University of Hawaii, occupies a 78-acre site along Kaahumanu Avenue midway between Kahului and Wailuku.

Central Maui Park will include an area from the west end of Kahului Harbor to Wailuku's edge. This proposed 190-acre park will incorporate the War Memorial recreational complex, housing for Maui Community College students, a cultural center and museum, harbor, Maui County Zoo, and sports and picnic areas.

Halekii and Pihana Heiau State Monument is reached from Waiehu Beach Road about 2 miles from Kahului; turn off on Kuhio Place, just past the bridge over Iao Stream, and follow the markers to the hilltop site. From the parking area, there's a good view down over central Maui and Kahului Harbor. Halekii, a 150 by 300-foot temple of worship, was used during the reign of Kahekili (1765–1795). A diagram at the site explains its partially restored stone walls, terraces, and

post holes. Pihana, 300 feet farther up at the end of a path, was a sacrificial temple consecrated in 1779.

Maui Jinsha, in Paukukalo off Highway 34, is a beautiful and fascinating Shinto shrine. Sacred objects are located in a separate little building; both it and the shrine have traditional roof symbols—protruding horns and a barrel-shaped ridge piece.

Wailuku~a mix of old and new

The best way to explore Wailuku's narrow, hilly streets is on foot. Many of the interesting new and old buildings are clustered in a compact area along High Street, between Main and Aupini streets. The Wailuku Historic District is on the west side of High Street. Walk some of the side streets to see older residential areas with small, tidy homes and colorful gardens. To view handsome homes on nicely landscaped hillside lots,

Tram stop on Maui Tropical Plantation tour allows time for refreshing nibble of pineapple, one of the island's main crops.

Kaahumanu Church was Maui's first Christian congregation. Present building dates from 1876.

drive up to Wailuku Heights; the road to it branches off the Iao Valley Road.

Government buildings line High Street. Most conspicuous is 9-story Kalana O Maui, the county office building. Adjacent to it, at the corner of High and Wells streets, sits the venerable 1907 Court House (the new building stands nearby). Federal offices occupy the building on the opposite corner of Wells Street; beyond, at High and Main streets, is the state office building.

The Wailuku Library, housed in an attractive, low, white stucco building on High Street across from the county office building, contains an excellent Hawaiiana room.

Kaahumanu Church, built on High Street in 1876 of plastered stone, is the third church building of Maui's first Christian congregation (1832). Its handsome spire, set off against a dramatic mountain backdrop, is a much-photographed subject.

Hale Hoikeike, off Iao Valley Road, is a museum consisting of two buildings: the home built in 1841 by Edward Bailey, head instructor of the Wailuku Female Seminary; and the kitchen–dining room of the school, an 1838–39 addition to its original building (now gone). The Bailey home has beams of hand-hewn sandalwood and 20-inch-thick stone walls covered with a mixture of plaster and goat hair. It contains historical exhibits, changing ethnic displays, and an exhibit of the 19th-century paintings of Edward Bailey.

The Church of the Good Shepherd, 2140 Main Street, is a 1911 Episcopal sanctuary of stone, with interior details of native woods and an unusual stained glass window behind the altar.

Wailuku Union Church, a small Gothic-style church on High Street, was built in 1911 to replace its 1867 predecessor.

Ka Lima O Maui, 95 Mahalani Street, is a rehabilitation center where you can buy Hawaiian crafts and nursery plants.

Iao Valley

From Wailuku you can drive for 3 miles into Iao Valley, never straying far from Iao Stream. The road (Highway 32) is a continuation of Wailuku's Main Street. Two miles from Wailuku, it passes Kepaniwai Heritage Gardens, a Maui County park with formal gardens and pavilions representing cultures that were instrumental to the growth of Hawaii. The name recalls a bloody battle fought here in 1790 in which Kamehameha I defeated the forces of the king of Maui. So many war-riors were killed, says the legend, that their bodies choked the stream. This gave the park its name—Kepaniwai—which means "damming of the waters."

The road ends in Iao Valley State Park, dominated by 2,250-foot Iao Needle, a green-mantled remnant of erosion that rises sharply for 1,200 feet from the north valley wall. From the parking lot at the end of the road, you can follow well-marked paths through an impressive collection of exotic plants and trees down to the stream, up to a shelter view spot for a look farther into the hushed ravine, and to the top of the ridge for a commanding vista of the Needle, the valley floor, and, in the distance, Kahului Bay.

Maui Tropical Plantation

At Waikapu, 3 miles south of Wailuku on Highway 30, this 60-acre plantation presents the story of Hawaiian agriculture in a unique and fascinating way. A tram takes you through acres of tropical crops—coffee, pineapple, guava, mango, and macadamia nuts. In the market and restaurant you have a chance to touch, sniff, and sample the delicious fruits you've seen in the fields. Open daily from 8 A.M. to 5 P.M., admission is free; there is a fee for the tram ride and for the lively luau held each Monday and Wednesday at 5:30 P.M. (reservations suggested).

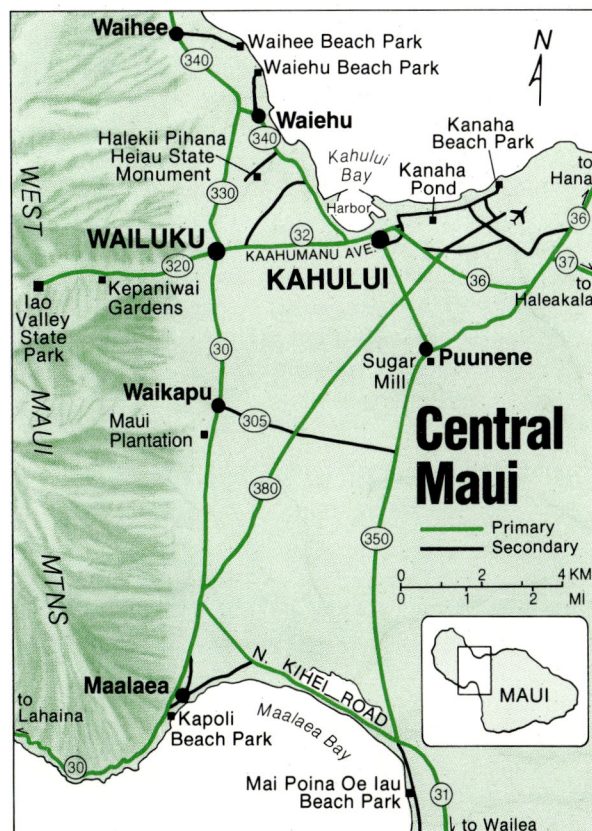

Central Maui

Lahaina/Kaanapali

This stretch of West Maui has for years been one of the most popular vacation destinations on the island. Devotees point out, quite rightfully, its scenic beauty and excellent beaches. Of at least equal importance are the well-preserved historical attractions which acquaint the visitor with the region's sometimes brawling and always fascinating past. Many vacationers (especially repeat ones) find everything they need or want right here and never stray far.

Kahului to Lahaina

From Kahului Airport, you'll drive about 6 miles on Highway 380 to its junction with Highway 30; from there, it's another 17 miles to Lahaina.

Shortly after you join Highway 30, a road veers left toward Maalaea, a settlement with several condominiums, stores, restaurants, and a wharf and boat harbor. There's a sweeping view across Maalaea Bay.

Highway 30 follows a picturesque route along the tops of seashore cliffs; at a scenic lookout, a plaque features information on the humpback whale, a seasonal visitor. The highway then descends to the narrow Olowalu plain, where cane fields slope up to mile-high mountains broken by Ukumehame Gulch and other deep gashes.

Monkeypod trees shade quiet Olowalu, a small community with a few homes, a fine French restaurant (Chez Paul), and a little general store that seems typically Hawaiian. A half mile to the north lies a good hunting ground for "Hawaiian diamonds" (high-grade quality). Surfing waves boom offshore here and also farther north at Launiupoko State Park.

Between Maalaea and Lahaina, Ukumehame and Puamana county parks and Papalaua and Launiupoko state parks are good places for a picnic.

Lahaina~Historic Waterfront Town

Modern Hawaiian history has its roots deeply embedded in Lahaina ("*cruel sun,*" as translated from early-day terminology). Kamehameha the Great established a residence here after he conquered Maui in a bloody battle in Iao Valley. Some of the first missionaries from Boston came ashore at Lahaina in 1823. And Kamehameha III lived here when he granted religious freedom and drew up Hawaii's first laws and constitution.

In the middle 1800s, whalers came by the thousands to winter in this little port, anchoring their ships offshore. Humpback whales migrating to their Hawaiian breeding grounds from the Aleutians still make whale watching a popular winter pastime. Tour boats leave from Lahaina and Maalaea harbors for a close-up look at these leviathans, some of which swim right up to the boats. The best months to see whales are January through April, though you may spot some stragglers as late as June.

Lahaina is still partly the town it has been for a century and a half—streets are narrow, sidewalks few, trees old and spreading, family gardens a tropical hodgepodge. Most houses are simple cottages. Some shopping still takes place in false-front wooden buildings.

But Lahaina no longer exists as it did more than 20 years ago, when its primary purpose was to sell staples

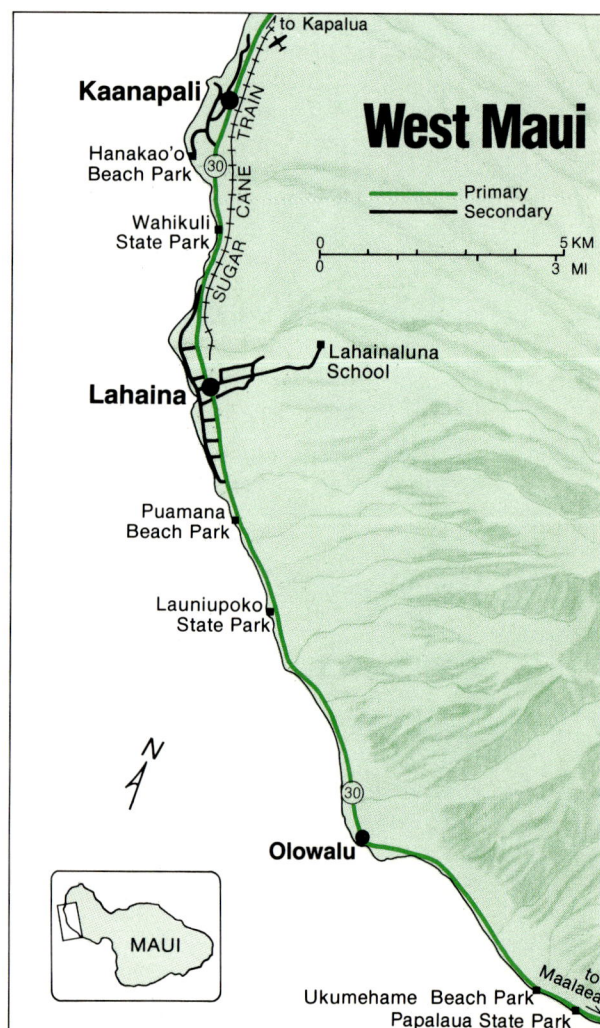

West Maui

to Kapalua

Kaanapali

Hanakao'o Beach Park

SUGAR CANE TRAIN

Wahikuli State Park

— Primary
— Secondary

0   5 KM
0   3 MI

Lahainaluna School

Lahaina

Puamana Beach Park

Launiupoko State Park

N

Olowalu

30

MAUI

to Maalaea

Ukumehame Beach Park
Papalaua State Park

to West Maui's cane and pineapple workers. New shopping complexes, restaurants, and bars (some in recycled buildings) are constantly being added to the scene. Today, Lahaina town is a popular and often crowded visitor destination.

Restoration activity. Lahaina is a national historic landmark, and its center is under Maui County Historic District protection.

Most of the additions and changes are in keeping with the town's restoration program, a joint effort of state and local government and the Lahaina Restoration Foundation. Weathered buildings (particularly on Front Street) are being refurbished and harmonious new building encouraged. Restoration and rebuilding are underway for a few structures from each period of Lahaina's 19th-century history—from early monarchy days through the beginnings of plantations and the influx of workers from the Orient. The famed old sea wall (a favorite place for watching sunsets) was restored in 1980. Wo Hing Temple on Front Street, built in 1912, underwent extensive renovation in the early 1980s (see page 15).

A walking town. Lahaina town is just the right size for walking. Nearly flat, it stretches out for 2 miles along the water but is only 4 blocks deep. Most of the historic places lie between Lahainaluna Road and Shaw Street (see pages 14–15) and are within a couple of blocks of Front Street; walking tour maps of Lahaina town are available at the Baldwin Home Museum.

You can cover most of Lahaina's in-town points of interest in about 1½ hours. If you have less time, explore the area along Front Street and the boat harbor, the departure point for fishing charters and a wide variety of boat cruises.

Night life. For those seeking evening entertainment, Lahaina offers musical sounds in several locations (check local papers for activities) and a general air of jollity. If you are visiting Maui in late October, don't miss the Halloween pageantry; just walking down Front Street is an experience you won't soon forget. To really get the most out of it, contrive a costume of some sort and join the celebration.

Lahaina to Kaanapali

The drive from Lahaina to Kaanapali on Highway 30 is short—less than 3 miles. The widened highway encourages cyclists. Just north of Lahaina, you can see the remains of a royal coconut grove, planted in 1827 by the wife of Maui's governor, Hoapila. Young palms are now taking the place of the older ones as they succumb to wind and age.

(Continued on page 17)

A Brief Hawaiian History

Lahaina's restoration offers a good look at Maui's history during the 1800s (see page 14). But Hawaii's beginnings date back to A.D. 500 when Polynesians from the Marquesas discovered the islands not by chance, but through impressive feats of navigation.

These explorers (and other Polynesians from Tahiti about 500 years later) crossed the uncharted ocean in large sailing canoes and landed in Hawaii with their families, plants, animals, and personal belongings. For hundreds of years, they knew only a Stone Age life, making *tapa* cloth, grass houses, outrigger canoes, and carvings. They subsisted on fish, poi, and other fruit of the land.

When British navigator Captain James Cook discovered the islands in 1778 (he named them the Sandwich Islands for the Earl of Sandwich) during the third and last of his famous South Pacific voyages, he found each a separate kingdom organized in a feudal manner—with chiefs, priests, and commoners.

By 1810 the king of Hawaii island, Kamehameha, had brought all of the islands under his domain. He and his descendants reigned until 1872. They were followed by rulers from another ancient family of chiefs that included Queen Liliuokalani, who was ruler in 1893 when the monarcy was overturned and a provisional government established.

The waves of immigrants who came during the 19th century rearranged Hawaiian society. In the middle years, whalers beached, seeking provisions and entertainment. Missionaries started arriving in 1820. These stern, dedicated New Englanders braved the hazardous journey to convert natives to Christianity and to introduce plantation agriculture, commerce, and democratic government. Many of their descendants are still prominent in the islands.

In the last half of the century came Chinese, then Portuguese and Japanese, and later on Filipinos to work the sugarcane and pineapple plantations started by early New Englanders.

On July 4, 1894, the Republic of Hawaii was established. The islands were annexed by the United States in 1898 and made a territory in 1900. Hawaii became the country's 50th state on March 12, 1959, ending a statehood campaign waged for nearly half a century.

A Stroll Through Lahaina's Past

Fortunate is the history buff who visits Lahaina, because here—in one compact area—the flavor of the past can be sampled in reasonable time and with minimum wear on the shoes. A publication containing expanded information about the historical attractions mentioned on these pages can be obtained from Baldwin Home or other museums.

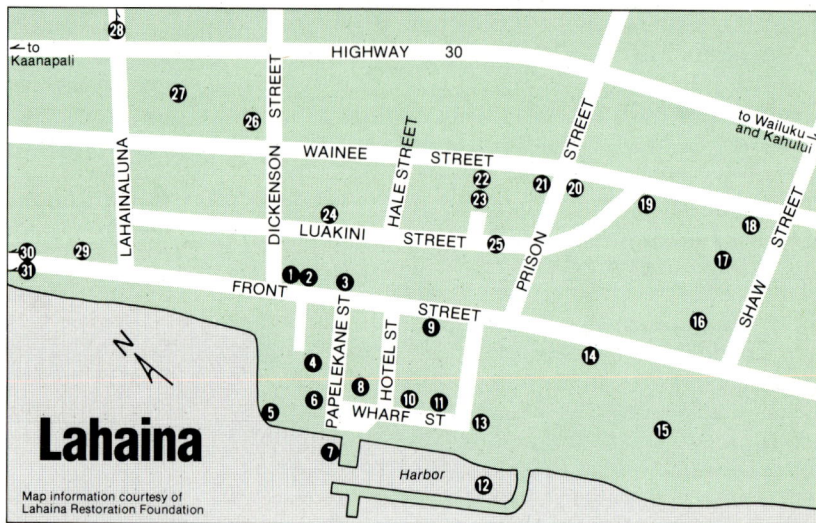

1. Masters' Reading Room, built in 1834 by missionaries and ships' officers, was restored by the Lahaina Restoration Foundation in 1970. Coral block and fieldstone construction was preserved.

2. Baldwin Home Museum includes Dr. Baldwin's dispensary-study and restored Baldwin Home, the New England style residence of medical missionary Dwight Baldwin and his family from 1836 to 1868. Built in 1834–35 of plastered coral and hand-hewn 'ohi'a beams, the home contains original furnishings and other period pieces. Dr. Baldwin's medical kit and theological books, and some early physicians' implements are displayed in the dispensary. The museum is open daily; there's an admission fee.

3. Site of Richards house, earliest coral stone house in the islands. William Richards was the first Protestant missionary to Lahaina. He traveled in the United States and Europe as envoy of Kamehameha III.

4. Site of taro patch, visible as late as the 1950s, where Kamehameha III once worked to show his subjects the dignity of labor.

5. Hauola Stone is believed to have been used by early Hawaiians as a healing place.

6. The "Brick Palace," thought to be the first Western-style building in the islands, was built at the command of Kamehameha I.

7. Carthaginian, a museum afloat, is a 93-foot replica of a 19th century brig. The ship contains a "World of the Whale" exhibit; there's an admission fee.

8. Pioneer Inn was west Maui's only visitor accommodation until the late 1950s. The original building was constructed in 1901; the amusing house rules of that time are posted in the rooms. A wing was added in 1964.

9. Banyan Tree, planted in 1873 to commemorate the 50th anniversary of the arrival of Lahaina's first Protestant missionaries, is the largest banyan in the islands. It covers an entire square (about two-thirds of an acre) behind the Courthouse. At sundown, mynah birds strike up a chorus you won't soon forget.

10. Courthouse was built in 1859 with stone from demolished Hale Piula (15).

11. Old Fort, next to the Courthouse, is a reconstruction of the ruins of a fort built here in the early 1830s and used chiefly to confine unruly seamen. The original fort was torn down in the 1850s to supply stones for the construction of Hale Paahao (21).

12. Harbor is not a natural one, as is Honolulu's. Whaling ships were forced to anchor in deep water offshore; smaller boats ferried the crews into town.

13. Site of old Government Market, where natives traded with sailors during the whaling days, is said to have earned its nickname: Rotten Row.

14. Holy Innocents' Episcopal Church was built in 1927; Episcopal services at Lahaina actually date back to 1862, when the first services were held in Hale Aloha. The church has a unique painting of the Madonna and Child for which a Lahaina mother and infant posed.

15. Site of Hale Piula, an old courthouse until damaged beyond repair by a gale in 1858. Its stones were used to build the present courthouse (10).

16. Maluuluolele Park was once the site of a pond with an island where several Maui chiefs were buried.

17. Wainee Church was the first stone church in the islands, circa 1830. Windstorms and fires have destroyed it several times since. The current church was renamed Waiola, "Water of Life."

18. Wainee Cemetery, planted with fragrant plumerias and ancient palms, has gravestones with inscriptions dating back to 1823. Keopuolani, queen of Kamehameha the Great, is buried here.

19. Hongwanji Mission has been a meeting place for Buddhists since 1910, when they erected a small temple. The present building dates from 1927.

20. Site of house of David Malo, renowned Hawaiian scholar and philosopher who fought hard to preserve old Hawaii against growing outside control. A graduate of Lahainaluna Seminary, his gravesite lies atop nearby Mt. Ball.

21. Hale Paahao, the old prison, has walls of coral block taken from the old waterfront fort (11).

22. Episcopal Cemetery contains the grave of Walter Murray Gibson, flamboyant and extravagant adviser to King Kalakaua in the 1880s.

23. Hale Aloha, built in 1858 and used as a church and school for many years, fell into ruins but was restored in 1974.

24. Shingon Buddhist Temple has the simple, wooden architectural style typical of houses of worship built during the plantation era when Japanese laborers were brought to Hawaii.

25. Luakini Street was the route of the funeral procession of Princess Nahienaena, who died tragically at age 21 in 1837.

26. Maria Lanakila Church was built in 1928. It replaced an 1858 frame structure established after the celebration of Maui's first Catholic Mass on Lahaina beach in 1841.

27. Seamen's Cemetery has only one inscribed marble slab and the fragment of another remaining. Buried here are a cousin and a shipmate of author Herman Melville.

28. Hale Pa'i and Lahainaluna School are across Highway 30 and 1½ miles up the hill. (Just before you begin the climb, you pass the old Pioneer Mill Company, which dates from 1860.) Hale Pa'i, a print shop at Lahainaluna Seminary founded by Protestant missionaries in 1831, produced Hawaiian textbooks and Hawaii's first newspaper. The school, the oldest educational institution west of the Rockies, now serves as the public high school for the Lahaina area. Hale Pa'i was restored in 1980–82. An exhibit features a replica of the early press and facsimiles of early printing. The museum is closed Sunday.

29. Wo Hing Temple is affiliated with the Chee Kung Tong, a Chinese fraternal society with branches all over the world. Recently restored, the temple has a small museum. The Chinese were among Hawaii's earliest immigrants and soon became a powerful force in commerce.

30. Seamen's Hospital was precisely that, during the whaling era from 1840 to 1865. But it also has served as a girl's school, vicarage, and residence—and once as a hideaway for Kamehameha III.

31. Jodo Mission contains the Japanese Cultural Park, commemorating the first immigrants. Here you'll find a giant bronze Buddha imported from Japan, a temple, pagodas, and a bell tower.

Buddha at Jodo Mission

Lahaina's historic Pioneer Inn

Kaanapali, Maui's first resort area, attracts visitors with deluxe resort hotels, premier golf courses, and miles of wide sandy beaches.

New England-style architecture serves as a reminder of Lahaina's past, a lusty period of whalers and missionaries.

Sugar Cane Train

One of the most unusual attractions in the islands is the 1890-style, open-sided train of the Lahaina Kaanapali & Pacific Railroad, which chugs along a 6-mile route, taking you back in time to the turn of the century when narrow-gauge trains were common on Hawaii's major islands.

The train runs on 36-inch, narrow-gauge, German-made tracks that were used by the Kahului Railroad before it stopped operating in 1966. It puffs its way through fields of sugarcane, crosses a 400-foot-long trestle, runs alongside the 4th hole of Kaanapali's south golf course (watch the golfers gawk!) and follows part of the roadbed of the cane haul line that traveled to and from Lahaina's Pioneer Mill between 1882 and 1952. As the train rolls along, passengers are entertained by a singing conductor.

Turn-of-the-century transportation

Cars with wooden seats are modeled after coaches that King Kalakaua had built to his order in England around 1888. The steam engine, "Anaka," incorporates parts of five early Hawaiian locomotives, including brass-trimmed domes and headlight and a mahogany cab. It and the backup engine, "Myrtle," were rebuilt to 1890–1910 vintage from derelict Porter locomotives sitting on track in Carbon, Ohio.

There are five scheduled departures daily from the Victorian-style stations at Lahaina and Kaanapali and the boarding platform at Puukolii. Earliest is 9:35 A.M. from Puukolii; last train, at 4:10 P.M. is one-way only from Lahaina to Puukolii. Tickets may be purchased at train stations or at tour and activities desks. Jitneys transport passengers to and from Lahaina town or the Kaanapali Beach hotels.

(Continued from page 13)

Two excellent beach parks, Wahikuli and Hanakaoo, are popular with local residents. Both offer sandy beaches, picnic tables, and changing rooms.

Kaanapali Beach Resort

As you approach the first of three entrance roads to the resort, you look out over the manicured greens and fairways of one of Kaanapali's two championship golf courses, the Kaanapali South Course. One clubhouse, just inside the turnoff, serves both the South and North courses. Parts of both courses climb to higher elevations and offer spectacular views.

The multifarious resort includes 600-plus developed acres and six deluxe beachfront hotels. Several condominiums face the ocean, and others flank the golf fairways. Kaanapali is a popular tennis center; most hotels and condominiums have courts. There are numerous restaurants, cocktail lounges, snack bars, swimming pools, shops, and a variety of nightly entertainment.

Free trolleys provide shuttle service around the resort, to and from the Sugar Cane Train's Kaanapali

Station (see above), and the Whalers Village and Museum. The latter, a multilevel, 8-acre complex of buildings and open plazas, combines displays of whaling artifacts with shops, art galleries, and eating places.

The Whalers Village Museum, in the center of the complex on the third floor of building G, houses perhaps the largest single collection of whaling memorabilia in existence. Your preview comes at the Whale Pavilion at the Kaanapali Parkway entrance to the center. Here you're greeted by the skeleton of a 40-foot sperm whale and scale models of many species of whales and dolphins.

From Whalers Village, an enjoyable barefoot walk lies along the beach past the Whaler and Kaanapali Beach hotels and up and over the Sheraton Black Rock to the northern beach of the Royal Lahaina Hotel. Here lie the ruins of the old Kaanapali Landing, an abandoned pier once used to ship out tons of sugar from cane fields on Kaanapali slopes.

Black Rock, where the Sheraton now stands, was once the home of the chief who ruled west Maui. Today, the turquoise ocean around the rock is a favorite snorkeling spot. The colorful reef fish, accustomed to visitors, appear almost tame.

With the arrival of winter each year, two groups of visitors make their presence known in Maui: the prime tourist season begins, and the humpback whales, having summered in Alaska and the Bering Sea, return to Maui's waters to breed, calve, and tend their young. First sightings usually occur in early December; by late May, all but a few stragglers will have departed.

The humpbacks are, to put it mildly, a sight to see. Once you've viewed them—particularly at close range from the deck of a whale-watcher cruise boat—you will begin to understand why the people of the islands have an ongoing love affair with these huge but gentle mammals. On page 46 you'll find a listing of boat trips, many of which include close-up views of the humpbacks. Look for the whale symbol.

The whale tale

Fewer than a thousand humpbacks remain in the North Pacific—about 600 of them visit Hawaii annually—but these are a small fraction of their numbers before they became prey to commercial

Maui's Friendly Visitors

hunters. Back in the mid-1800s, when as many as 450 whaling ships anchored in Lahaina each winter, perhaps 15,000 humpbacks inhabited the North Pacific. Though protected by international convention since 1966, the humpback population continues to decline. Both the Pacific Whale Foundation, headquartered in Maui, and the University of Hawaii are devoted to research, conservation, and education programs focused on whales (also dolphins and porpoises).

Humpbacks are 10 to 15 feet long at birth, weighing from 1 to 3 tons. During the first few weeks they gain about 200 pounds a day, due largely to the high percentage of fat in the mother's milk. When full sized, they average 45 feet in length, often weighing over 40 tons. Their long flukes (tails) have markings under-

neath which differ with each humpback; researchers who track their comings and goings can identify each individual from these "fingerprints."

Scientists have revealed that some male humpbacks "sing," or at least produce noises ranging from shrieks to low growling sounds that travel for miles in the water. Research continues as to what this might signify.

What to watch for

Whale watchers soon learn the meanings of four key terms: "breaching," "spy hopping," "fluking," and "fluke-slapping."

A whale "breaches" when it comes bursting out of the water head-first—maybe because it's disturbed about something or perhaps just having fun. If you see part of the whale's head out of the water for more than a couple of seconds, it's "spy hopping"—having a look-see above the surface. "Fluking" means that the whale is diving; the tail emerges and quickly submerges again. If its tail slaps against the surface in the process (an awesome "thwack"), the whale is "fluke-slapping."

Breaching humpback whale

Northwest Maui

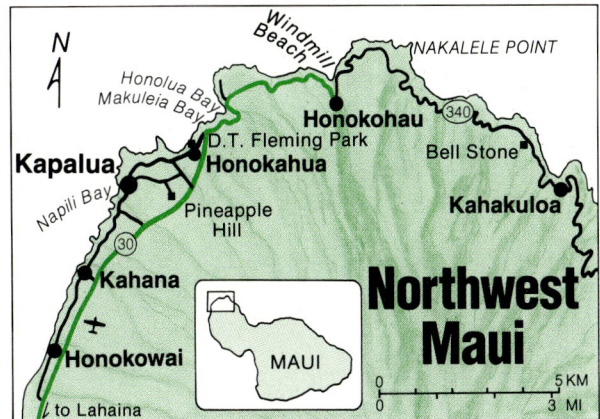

Less than a 10-minute drive north from Kaanapali, two vacation destinations attract an increasing number of visitors each year: Napili Bay and Kapalua. These adjacent regions have their own special characteristics, yet the two areas share at least one important asset—a spectacular view across brilliant blue ocean to the neighboring islands of Molokai and Lanai.

For those who enjoy auto exploring, the rugged north coast is right "next door."

Kaanapali to Napili Bay

North of Kaanapali, Highway 30 takes an inland route above the apartments, condominiums, and cottages lining both sides of the lower road, which travels through Honokawai to Kahana before joining the highway. A little more than a mile farther you come to Napili. Several condominiums and informal resorts with kitchen facilities preside over a lovely curve of sandy beach.

Kapalua Resort

Just to the north of Napili lies Kapalua Resort, one of the island's primary vacation destinations since its inception in the mid-1970s. The Kapalua Bay Hotel, the resort's central feature, stands just back from Kapalua Beach. There are also several vacation villas and residential communities.

Kapalua's 750 landscaped acres include two 18-hole golf courses. The Village Course, opened for play in 1981, combines a challenging hillside layout with dramatic views from just about anywhere. Kapalua's original golf links, the Bay Course, ranges from the lower slopes down to the water's edge and features tropical landscape planting.

Tennis courts are located in a secluded garden area. Kapalua Bay offers plentiful water sports—windsurfing, scuba diving, snorkeling, and just plain swimming. Riding stables are only a 5-minute drive away, at Rainbow Ranch.

Kapalua to Honokahua

Beyond Kapalua Bay are several excellent beaches favored—and sometimes nicknamed—by local people: Oneloa (Beach Camp) Beach; D. T. Fleming Park (Ball Park or Stable Point), fronting 600 feet of white sand *makai* of Honokahua village (swimming and surfing for experts only); Makuleia Bay (Slaughterhouse Beach); and Honolua Bay. Because of their wealth of underwater life, Makuleia Bay and most of Honolua Bay have been designated by the state as a marine life conservation district.

Around the West Maui Mountains

The narrow, twisting, up-and-down road around the north end of the West Maui Mountains follows the course of an old royal horse trail and bears the extravagant title "Kahekili Highway." Highway 340 isn't a good wet-weather drive; pavement ends just 5 miles east of Honokohau Bridge and begins again about 2 miles farther. Check insurance coverage with your car rental agency before making the trip.

Between the island's north point and Honokohau, you cross weathered sandstone bluffs of various hues. There's a blowhole on the jagged coast. Windmill Beach, usually windy and rough, is splendid for diving on glassy days.

Honokohau is a jungle of fruit trees. Drive down into the valley a little way to see taro cultivated beside the stream and orchids on the slope. Just before you dip down into Kahakuloa village, try to get a ring from a rockside boulder known as the Bell Stone; you're supposed to listen on one side while someone bangs a rock against the other. (Results are dubious, but the stone is well worn from many trial bangs.)

Kahakuloa village stands at the mouth of a green valley in the middle of cattle country; a bold headland guards the southern approach. Amid the cluster of iron-roofed, wooden shacks fringed by a patchwork of taro, you'll find two picturesque churches—one Catholic and one Protestant. Villagers still pound poi, raise pigs, fish, beat the washing on rocks in the stream—but, at night, watch television.

Beyond Kahakuloa, the road winds along cliffs above fern gulches that stretch to the sea.

Maui's Best Beaches & Swimming Holes

A temperate climate with year-round sun and gentle breezes, sparkling water, miles of spectacular sand, and normally gentle surf make the Valley Isle a good choice for anyone who enjoys life at the beach. Beginning on page 44, you'll find a listing of water sports activities—from surfing, snorkeling, and scuba diving to boating and deep-sea fishing.

For those who simply like to swim or walk along the water's edge, the beaches listed below include some of the island's best stretches. Most are found on the leeward side.

All of the state's beaches are publicly owned and most have a right-of-way access. Only developed beaches provide parking areas. Larger beaches offer a variety of facilities including restrooms and picnic tables.

Though Maui's beaches are among the best in the world, you should heed a few simple rules for the most enjoyable outing:

- To avoid wrecking your vacation with a sunburn, expose yourself gradually to Hawaii's tropical sun. An hour at midday may be too much for fair-skinned people. Protect your skin with a good suntan lotion.
- Inquire locally about the safety of a beach—currents, tides, and drop-offs —before entering the water.
- Duck or dive *beneath* breaking waves just before they reach you.
- Coral cuts are easily infected. Avoid swimming or snorkeling near coral in shallow water. Protect your feet with sneakers or similar gear when walking on reefs.
- Don't get mesmerized when snorkeling—you may suddenly find yourself far offshore.

- If you get in trouble in the water, concentrate on staying afloat until help arrives; remain calm and don't waste your breath with pointless yelling.
- Never turn your back on the ocean when you are near the shoreline.
- Never swim alone.

Swimming

You'll find safe swimming at the spots listed below, but always stay alert for such adverse conditions as strong tides or high winter surf. Unlisted beaches may be dangerous; watch for posted warnings. One of the best ways to check out the safety of a beach is to look for local residents. If they are not in the water, ask why before you jump in.

For detailed descriptions of all of Maui County's beaches (includes Lanai and Molokai), pick up a copy of *The Beaches of Maui County* by John R. K. Clark (The University Press of Hawaii, Honolulu) at a bookstore on the island.

Ocean swimming

Waihee Beach Park, Waihee
Kapalua Beach, Kapalua
Napili Bay, Napili
Keonenui Beach, Alaeloa
Kahana Beach, Kahana
Honokowai Beach Park, Honokowai
Kaanapali Beach, Kaanapali
Hanakaoo Beach, Kaanapali
Wahikuli State Wayside Park, Wahikuli
Puamana Beach Park, Lahaina
Launiupoko State Wayside Park
(includes a manmade ocean pool), Launiupoko
Kulanaokalai Beach, Kulanaokalai
Awalua Beach, Awalua
Mai Poina Oe Iau Beach Park, Kihei
Kalepolepo Beach, Kalepolepo
Kamaole Beach Parks I, II, III, Kamaole
Keawakapu Beach, Keawakapu

Mokapu Beach, Wailea
Ulua Beach, Wailea
Poolenalena Beach, Poolenalena
Oneuli Beach, Puuolai
Hana Beach Park, Hana

Freshwater swimming

Swimmers will also discover some of the state's most picturesque swimming holes along the highway to Hana and beyond. We've included some of the favorite freshwater spots.

Seven Pools Park, Kipahulu
Waianapanapa Cave, Waianapanapa State Park
Ulaino Stream
Hinamoo Pool in Nahiku Stream, Puaakaa State Park
Keanae Stream
Twin Falls, Hana Highway

Beachcombing, tidepooling, & reef walking

An interesting cross section of Maui's underwater environment is yours for the viewing as you stroll through shallow waters. Wear canvas shoes for lava or reef walking; gloves are also a good precaution. Leave rocks as you find them; exposure to light kills some marine life.

Low-tide walking sites

Kahului Bay, Kahului
Waiehu Beach Park, Waiehu
Waihee Beach Park, Waihee
Olowalu Beach, Olowalu
Makena Bay, Makena
Nuu Bay, Kaupo
Seven Pools Park, Kipahulu
Hana Beach Park, Hana
H. A. Baldwin Park, Spreckelsville

Southwest Maui

Until the early 1970s, Maui's southwest coast—from Maalaea Bay through Kihei and on south to Makena—was a quiet rural area where the only break in the lazy routine was a visit to Azeka's store, the post office, or Kihei's original and still charming resort, the low-rise Maui Lu. But, with its exceptional weather and multiplicity of excellent beaches, this region was destined to become the major tourist destination that it is today. It seems—to local residents who remember a kiawe-tree-covered area where seldom was heard the sound of a jackhammer—to have happened almost overnight.

This part of Maui is dry and usually sunny, receiving less than 10 inches of rainfall annually. Had it not been for the scarcity of water, tourism would have come to the region much earlier. When plans were laid for the Wailea resort area just south of Kihei, a major project was undertaken to import water from the rainy West Maui Mountains. By the early 1970s, condominiums and apartment hotels were under construction all along the coast; this development has continued, not only near the water but inland to the lower slopes of Haleakala.

Maalaea

If, on arrival at Kahului Airport, you wish to proceed to the increasingly popular Maalaea region, pick up Highway 380 just southwest of the terminal. Follow it almost all the way across the island's "saddle" until the junction with Highway 30. Take Highway 30 for a short distance, then veer left on the road which leads to Maalaea Harbor.

Until recent years, Maalaea consisted of not much more than a wharf, a boat harbor, and the long-popular Buzz's Wharf restaurant; the area now has a growing number of condominiums, all of them on or near the ocean.

Not the least of Maalaea's appealing features is its "hub" location—only a few minutes' drive from the attractions of Lahaina/Kaanapali/Kapalua to the northwest, Wailuku/Kahului to the northeast, and Kihei/Wailea/Makena to the south.

Kihei

Highway 350 from Kahului Airport crosses central Maui from ocean to ocean; the drive takes about 25 minutes, depending on traffic conditions. Along the way you pass through miles of cane fields, with views of Maui's two mountain masses on either side—Haleakala to the

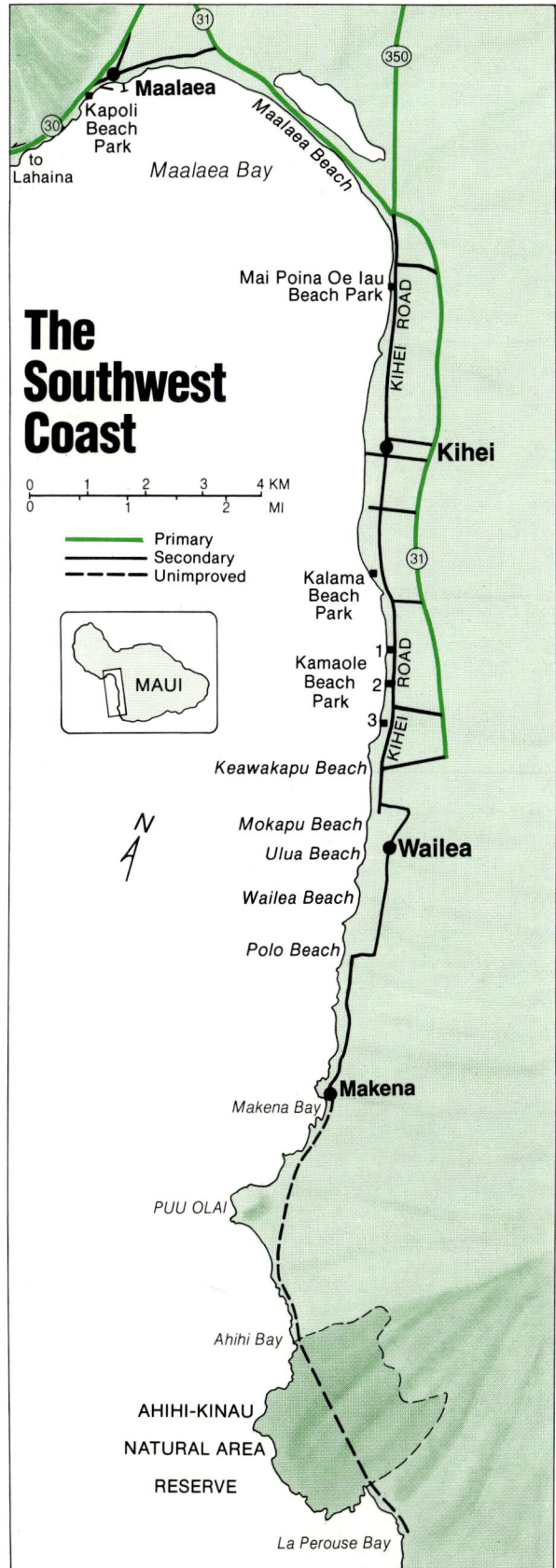

The Southwest Coast

0 1 2 3 4 KM
0 1 2 MI

—— Primary
—— Secondary
- - - Unimproved

MAUI

N

Maalaea
Kapoli Beach Park
to Lahaina
Maalaea Bay
Maalaea Beach
Mai Poina Oe Iau Beach Park
KIHEI ROAD
Kihei
Kalama Beach Park
Kamaole Beach Park 1 2 3
KIHEI ROAD
Keawakapu Beach
Mokapu Beach
Ulua Beach
Wailea
Wailea Beach
Polo Beach
Makena
Makena Bay
PUU OLAI
Ahihi Bay
AHIHI-KINAU NATURAL AREA RESERVE
La Perouse Bay

left, the West Maui Mountains to the right. Kihei is most easily reached by following the highway all the way to Kihei Road, which runs the gamut of condominiums south along the ocean to the Wailea Resort turnoff. For a more direct route to Wailea, turn left from Highway 350 shortly before it reaches the ocean, onto the newer and faster Highway 31. You can also take this route to Kihei: several turnoffs lead to Kihei Road. Or, if you are staying at the extreme southern end of Kihei, turn *makai* (toward the ocean) when you reach Wailea and then buttonhook back on Kihei Road.

For sunny weather, sandy beaches, and good ocean swimming, Kihei and the areas just north and south of it cannot be topped anywhere else on the island—or, for that matter, anywhere in Hawaii. Beach parks along this coast are popular with visitors and local residents alike. Reserve Kalama Park's pavilions in advance; they're usually crowded with festive groups on weekends and holidays. Kamaole Beach Park, just to the south, actually includes three separate beaches, with picnic tables, showers, and changing rooms.

A popular family vacation destination, Kihei has dozens of condominiums to choose from, for just about any budget. Spaced throughout the region are several excellent restaurants and shopping centers.

Wailea Resort

One of Maui's three world-famed luxury resorts, this 1,450-acre complex includes the Inter-Continental and Stouffer's Wailea Beach hotels, four condominium villages, private homes, five beaches, shops, and restaurants. Guests enjoy tennis, volleyball, snorkeling, sailing, windsurfing, scuba diving, and lessons in hula. Three of its 14 tennis courts are grass—hence Wailea's nickname of "Wimbledon West."

There are two scenic and challenging 18-hole golf courses, the Blue (original) and the demanding Orange. The straight-growing trees on both courses are signs of exceptional year-round golf weather, generally free from blustery winds.

Makena

South of Wailea, the road continues to Makena. In the days when Ulupalakua Ranch was planted with sugarcane, the area contained Maui's second-ranking port. Until recent years a quiet settlement by the sea, Makena now is home to the luxurious Maui Prince Hotel, an oceanside complex of low-rise condominiums, and a challenging 18-hole golf course designed by Robert Trent Jones, Jr.

Five beaches accessible by regular car are, north to south: Poolenalena, Maluaka, Oneuli, Puuolai, and Oneloa. All are swimmable, but safest are Poolenalena, Maluaka, and Puuolai.

In a 4-wheel-drive vehicle, you can continue on a rocky, rutty road down the coast to La Perouse Bay, named for the French explorer who anchored here in 1786 and then sailed away to mysteriously disappear at sea.

Ahihi-Kinau Natural Area Reserve encompasses the south end of Ahihi Bay and Cape Kinau. This ecologically important area has been set aside by the state to protect and preserve its unique natural resources. The lava flows forming Cape Kinau resulted from Maui's last volcanic activity, estimated to have occurred in 1790. Unusual species of marine life thrive in the reserve's tidal pools and offshore waters. The ruins of Moanakala, a small fishing village, are a focus for anthropological research.

Driving Tips

Driving a car in Maui can be a very pleasurable experience. It helps, though, to understand some of the important features of driving in the islands.

- Most of Maui's roads are narrow, two-lane affairs. It's advisable—if you have a choice—to rent a compact rather than a full-size car.
- Never go faster than the posted speed limit and, equally important, don't drive too slowly: this invites impatient drivers behind you to pass, risking head-ons.
- If cars press from behind, pull over at a safe place and let them go by.

- Look out for passing cars coming toward you. The road between Maalaea and Lahaina can be particularly dangerous.
- Go easy on the horn. Hawaii's people don't take kindly to honking, considering it a breach of the aloha spirit.
- Obey yield signs; if you don't, you can find yourself in trouble, particularly on the road to Hana with its many narrow bridges.

- Make sure the blades in your windshield wipers are in good shape; rains can be heavy, and frequent.
- If you drive up to the high country and have trouble restarting your car after a short stop (a variety of reasons can cause this), wait a few minutes, then try the starter again before looking under the hood or calling a garage—chances are good that the car will start.
- Don't drive on unimproved roads unless you have a 4-wheel-drive vehicle; if your car gets stuck, it's expensive to get it pulled out.

*Enjoying a quiet moment, family wades along edge of
palm-fringed beach near Kalama Park in Kihei.*

Upcountry

When you head up the slopes of Haleakala from Kahului, you move into a different Hawaii. Though a favorite of islanders, this part of Maui is, unfortunately, overlooked by many visitors. The weather is cooler here than at sea level—a desirable trait to some island residents.

Upcountry gardens are usually ablaze with colorful, temperate-zone flowers. Cattle graze in lush pastureland, and farmers grow many kinds of vegetables—including cucumbers, tomatoes, most of the state's cabbage crop, and sweet Kula onions (perhaps the pride of the region). Groves of eucalyptus dot the green hillsides, soft clouds drift in and out of valleys and swirl over the higher slopes, and the views down over the isthmus and out to the coast are magnificent. In spring, jacaranda trees are strung with purple blossoms.

You can sample upcountry Maui on the drive to Haleakala National Park along highways 37, 377, and 378. To see the heart of the big Kula district, continue on Highway 37 to Kula Hospital and Ulupalakua Ranch. But the best way to explore the upcountry is to drive some of the side roads. Maui maps don't always show them, but almost any road will carry you through a refreshingly rural countryside where the pace is slow, the people friendly, and the scenery restful. The road from Keokea to Kula Hospital has some exceptionally beautiful plantings just before you reach the hospital buildings.

Many of Hawaii's best-known families have year-round or part-time homes upcountry, especially in the southern region generally referred to as Kula. Early settlers, mostly farmers and plantation workers, came from China, Japan, and the Portuguese islands of Madeira and the Azores.

An Ethnic Duo

Kula's treasure, the octagonal Church of the Holy Ghost, reflects this heritage: the original parishioners of this 1897 Catholic church were mostly Portuguese. Perched on the hillside above the highway near Waiakoa, the church and its delicate steeple can be seen from many directions. If it's open, go inside to admire the gilded wooden bas-reliefs and the large, Austrian-made altar shipped in sections around Cape Horn.

Another example of the area's multiethnic heritage is St. John's Episcopal Church in Keokea, once a thriving Chinese community. The church was founded by a Chinese Lutheran minister who taught Chinese language and culture to the immigrants' children; the name of the church appears in Chinese characters

(Continued on page 27)

Since the late 1970s, upcountry Maui, with its rich volcanic soil, has been the locale for one of Hawaii's burgeoning agricultural-floral pursuits—the growing of proteas. These astonishingly diverse South African natives belong to a plant family comprised of about 1,500 varieties—hence the name (say PRO-tee-uh), after the Greek god who was noted for his ability to change shape at will. (Macadamia nuts, another booming crop in Maui, are a protea relative.) The plants, which have flowers that look like pearl-colored artichokes, day-glow pincushions, or neon sea anemones, thrive on the rich, acidic soil.

Protea blooms, with many colors to choose from, make superb cut flowers that hold their hue for weeks and retain their shape even after fading. They are easy to dry; simply hang them upside down for two to three weeks.

Protea~ An Exotic

Spectacular and durable

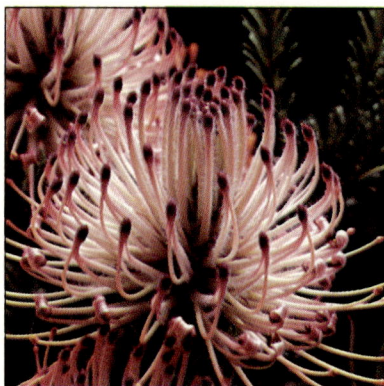

Upcountry growers concentrate on varieties with large and exotic flowers which shippers then proceed to process and package for mailing.

Several of the farms have stands where you can have fresh-cut flowers or small seedlings shipped back to the mainland. Prices for the cut flowers vary depending on number and variety of blooms. Expect to pay around $25–$30 for a selection. Several farms offer Christmas wreaths, which can be dried so they last for years.

Good places to see the flowers and learn how they are grown are Protea Cooperative of Hawaii near the Kula Post Office, Upcountry Protea Farm on Upper Kimo Drive near Kula Lodge, Sunrise Protea Farm on Highway 378 (2 miles from Highway 377), and Protea Gardens of Maui Flower Shoppe on Highway 377. You'll find other farms on byways.

Hard-riding paniolos, born to the saddle and proud of their heritage, are an exhilarating part of the upcountry scene.

Easy paths wind through acres of plantings at Kula Botanical Garden in Maui's quiet upland. Picnic tables invite you to enjoy the sweeping views.

Historic Ulupalakua Ranch, on Haleakala's southwest slope, encompasses 18,000 acres of the most scenic and pastoral country you are likely to see anywhere. Back in the 1850s and 1860s, James Makee (the erstwhile captain of a whaling ship) grew sugarcane here; he probably never dreamed that Ulupalakua would one day become one of the largest working cattle ranches on the island. And—though upcountry Maui turned out small quantities of wine for Hawaiian royalty even in the last century—Makee never could have envisioned Ulupalakua's producing Hawaii's first commercial grape wine with possibilities for eventual worldwide distribution.

A lengthy but scenic drive

Ulupalakua (accent the first and last "u") is reached via Highway 37, east of Kahului. The drive takes a while; if you are coming from western Maui or Kihei/Wailea, plan on 1½ to 2 hours each way.

More than compensating for the length of the trip is the ever-changing scenery of oceanscapes, cane fields, the West Maui Mountains, Haleakala, colorful flower gardens, picturesque small farms and ranches, and—when you get to the Kula region—sweeping views of the southwest coast and the impressive (if forlorn) bulk of the uninhabited island of Kahoolawe.

Short minutes after you proceed southwest from Keokea, Ulupalakua's verdant grazing lands come into view up the slope of Haleakala to your left. This was once exclusively cattle land, but, in very recent years, sheep (grown for meat, rather than wool) have been added to the scene. They, like the vineyards soon visible on your right, indicate that diversification has become not only advisable but essential to the area's cattle ranches.

Though the ranchlands continue up to about 6,500 feet, most of Ulupalakua's acreage extends down the southwest slope to sea level. As altitude decreases, rains become less frequent; grassy meadows and lush plantings gradually give way to scrubby growth, *kiawe* trees, and even cactus.

Ulupalakua~ Paniolos & Champagne

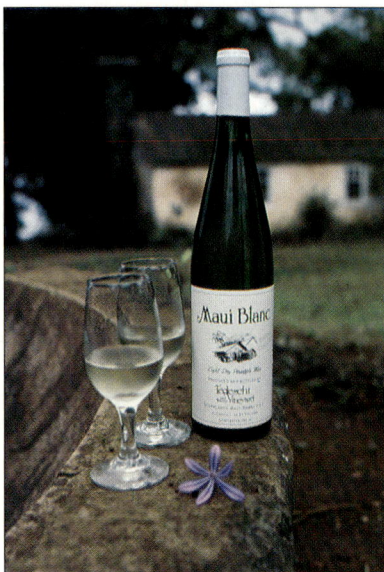

White wine, Maui-style

Paniolos~old Maui on horseback

If you keep an alert eye while driving through the cattle country, you may be treated to the sight of *paniolos* (Hawaiian cowboys) at work on the range. No place in upcountry Maui, or perhaps anywhere else, does the cowboy have a more distinguished tradition than at Ulupalakua.

More than 150 years ago, three Spanish-Mexican cowboys arrived in Hawaii, brought over from California by King Kamehameha III to control foraging cattle and begin raising them for beef. Islanders called them paniolos, the Hawaiian equivalent of *Españoles*. The Hawaiians themselves soon became paniolos, learning from the three "originals." Today, there are still a few paniolos working Ulupalakua whose fathers, grandfathers, and great-grandfathers rode the range many years before them.

Hawaii's "Napa Valley"?

The idea of a commercial vineyard at Ulupalakua was the concurrent dream of not one person but two: C. Pardee Erdman, owner of the ranch, and Emil Tedeschi, a young man who learned first hand about wine making while growing up in California's famed Napa Valley and was convinced that the climate and rich volcanic soil of upcountry Maui were exceptionally well suited to wine grapes. (To quote Tedeschi: "Napa Valley may be God's Country, but upcountry Maui is surely His vacation spot.")

In 1973, the two men went into partnership and began a venture that was to result, 10 years later, in 2,000 cases of Hawaii's first home-grown commercial wine. Four years of experimentation with 140 varieties of grapes were necessary in order to decide on the one best suited to the 2,000-foot elevation: Carnelian, a deep red hybrid of Cabernet Sauvignon, Grenache, and Carignane grapes.

The first Hawaiian wines

Having been advised that Carnelian could make not only red wine but a sparkling white, the partners opted for a champagne as their first commercial product (it has a faint blush of pink). On December 15, 1983, Tedeschi and Erdman hosted a formal celebration at the winery to celebrate Hawaii's entry into the world of grape wine.

Next, from the 1985 harvest, came two wines—Maui Blush and Maui Nouveau. Helping to ease the financial picture somewhat during the winery's struggling early years has been a popular and profitable pineapple wine, Maui Blanc, introduced by Tedeschi in 1977.

In at least one respect, Tedeschi Winery is distinct from wineries on the mainland and elsewhere: It uses an old jail (1856) for a tasting room. Thick lava walls and shade from an ancient camphor tree keep it sufficiently cool for wine storage. (A trap door leads down to the dungeon, which is cooler yet.)

If you don't have a car but would like to visit the winery, check with a travel agency or at a hotel desk; van tours stop at the tasting room en route to Hana.

(Continued from page 24)

over the doorway. If you bring a picnic, nearby Keokea Park is a pleasant place to stop.

A Garden Quartet

The University of Hawaii College of Tropical Agriculture operates two experiment stations on Haleakala's slopes: one of 20 acres in Kula and another, 34 acres, near Makawao. To reach the Kula station, turn off Highway 37 on Copp Road, just south of Kula Elementary School, and follow the signs. The terraced plantings include new varieties of bedding plants, All-America award-winning roses, and a rare collection of ornamental proteas (see special feature on page 24). The Makawao station specializes in macadamias and avocados. Macadamia nut trees, more and more plentiful in parts of the islands, now grow on some of Maui's acreage that formerly was cane fields.

If plants and flowers interest you, a visit to Kula Botanical Garden on Highway 377 offers a highly pleasurable experience. There are more than 700 types of plants. Easy paths wind between the beds; a picnic table and various resting places invite you to relax and admire a sweeping view beyond the landscaped slopes. Maui Enchanting Gardens (Highway 37 on the way to Kula Hospital) is a similar garden delight.

Auto Exploring

For the back-country explorer, an unimproved road climbs 10½ miles from Highway 377 to Polipoli Spring State Recreation Area at the edge of a mixed conifer and hardwood forest. A car with four-wheel drive is best for this trip. You can hike 1,000 feet to the top of Polipoli cinder cone, a Haleakala ridge vantage point from which you can see west Maui and the islands of Kahoolawe and Hawaii. The forest, with hiking trails, contains approximately 35,000 redwoods planted in 1927, some now 4 feet in diameter and 80 feet tall. A low-cost cabin in the recreation area can be reserved through the State Parks office in Wailuku (see page 55).

Near the end of Highway 370, on a shoulder above the road, you'll find a Hawaiian sacred boulder to which offerings are sometimes still made. According to legend, the boulder is a man turned into lava by Pele, the volcano goddess, whom he had angered.

Highway 370 officially ends at parklike Ulupalakua Ranch (see page 26). If you keep going past Ulupalakua, you'll be on Highway 31 going south and then eastward along the coast as far as Hana. (This route is described, coming from Hana, on page 39.)

For a pleasant, little-traveled route from Kula back down to the Wailuku-Kahului area, turn west from Highway 37 onto Pulehu Road (about 3 miles south of Pukalani); it comes out near Puunene Mill.

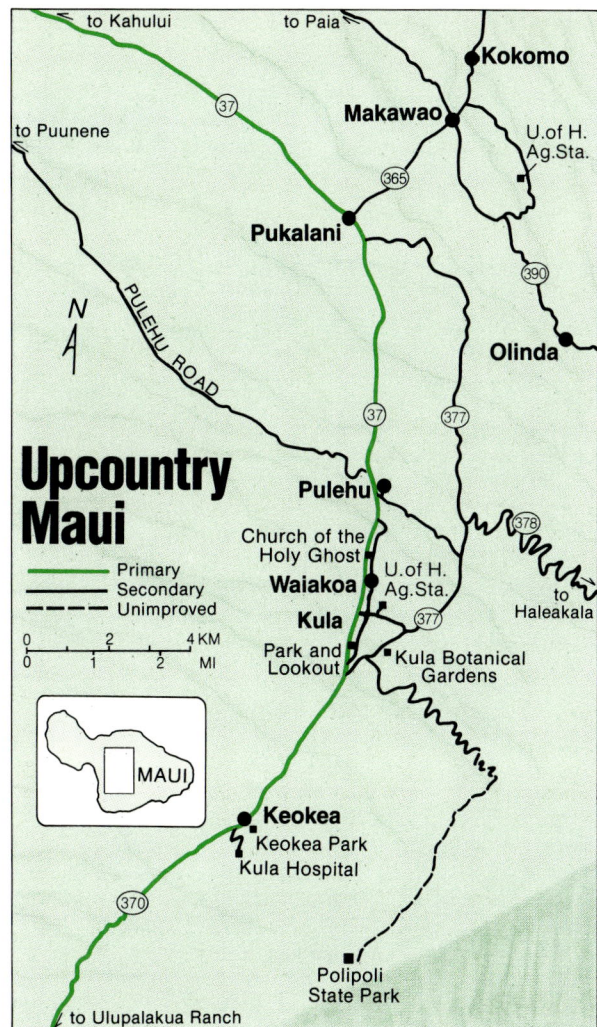

Upcountry Maui

— Primary
– – Secondary
- - - Unimproved

Makawao. To see another part of Haleakala's slopes, take Highway 365 from Pukalani junction on Highway 37 to Makawao, the spiritual center of Maui cow country. This village once bustled with field hands and upcountry *paniolos* (Hawaiian cowboys), and experienced a boom when nearby Kokomo served as a Marine base during World War II. Although the town is quieter today, it is much more than just boarded-up doorways and dogs snoozing in the sunshine.

Outside of town, subdivisions continue to spring up with the usual, unavoidable subtle changes in the town itself. There is much interest in crafts, now, and in fashions other than "wild west."

From Makawao, you can drive uphill on Highway 39 to Olinda, past Pookela Church, built of coral by missionaries in 1850, and Seabury Hall, an exclusive college preparatory and boarding school. Going downhill, you reach Paia by continuing down Baldwin Avenue, Makawao's main street, or Haiku by taking the Kokomo and Haiku roads.

The New Words You'll Hear

As you might expect, the English spoken in the islands has been augmented with words and expressions from languages native to Hawaii's various ethnic groups. You'll hear people pronounce vowel sounds in English words as they would in Hawaiian, Japanese, or one of the Romance languages.

You'll also hear pidgin English—shortcut communicating that may be unintelligible. Most islanders can and usually do speak good English; they just enliven their talk with Hawaiian words and occasionally interject pidgin vocabulary.

Since names of most places and streets are Hawaiian, some knowledge of the pronunciation rules of this language will prove helpful. The Hawaiian alphabet contains only 12 letters: the 5 vowels plus 7 consonants (h, k, l, m, n, p, and w). Words seem to overflow with vowels, but pronunciation is not difficult if you remember to pronounce every letter separately. The vowel sounds are *a* as in "arm," *e* as in "end," *i* as in "machine," *o* as in "old," and *u* as in "rude." Consonants have the same sounds as in English except for the *w*. Some Hawaiians always pronounce it as a *v* unless it is preceded by an *o* or *u*; others do so only when it is the next to last letter in a word. In diphthongs (*ei, eu, oi, ou, ai, ae, ao, au*), stress the first member (*lei*).

If you see a glottal stop mark, or hamza, it indicates, in the Polynesian language, that the letter *k* has been omitted; there is a definite break in sound between the letters it separates.

Here are some frequently used words and phrases. You'll hear other words in conversations with local residents. Some of the words below are not pure Hawaiian.

'ae	yes
ahui ho	until we meet again
ahupua'a	land division
aikane	friend (slang)
'aina	land, earth
akamai	wise, smart
ala	road, path
ali'i	royalty, a chief
aloha	greetings, welcome, farewell, love
aloha nui loa	much love
'a'ole	no
auwe	alas! ouch
ha'ina	end of song
hale	house
hana	work
hana hou	encore
haole	Caucasian
hapa	half, part
hapai	to carry, be pregnant
Hauoli la Hanau	Happy Birthday
Hauoli Makahiki Hou	Happy New Year
heiau	temple
hele mai	come here
hikie'e	large couch
holoku	fitted ankle-length dress with train
holomu'u	fitted ankle-length dress
ho'olaule'a	celebration
huhu	angry
hui	club, association
hukilau	to fish with a seine
iki	small, little
ipo	sweetheart, lover
kahili	feather standard
kahuna	priest, expert
kai	sea
kala	money
kama'aina	native born
kanaka	person, man
kanalua	doubtful, hesitant
kane	male, husband
kapakahi	crooked, lopsided
kapu	forbidden, keep out
kaukau	food (slang)
keiki	child
kokua	help
kona	lee side
kuleana	right, property, responsibility
kumu	teacher
lanai	porch, veranda
lei	garland, wreath
lomi (or *lomilomi*)	rub, press, massage
lua	toilet
mahalo	thanks
maika'i	good, fine
makai	toward the sea
make	dead
malihini	stranger, newcomer
malo	a loin cloth
manu	bird
manuahi	free, gratis
mauka	inland
mauna	mountain
mele	song
Mele Kalikimaka	Merry Christmas
menehune	dwarf, legendary race of dwarfs
moana	ocean
moemoe	sleep (slang)
momona	fat
mu'umu'u	long or short loose-fitting dress
nani	beautiful
ne'i	this place
nui	big, large, great
ohana	family
'okolehao	ti-root liquor
'okole maluna	bottoms up
'ono	delicious, tasty
'opu	belly, stomach
Pake	Chinese (slang)
pali	cliff, precipice
paniolo	cowboy
pau	finished
pa'u	wrap-around skirt
pehea 'oe	how are you?
pikake	jasmine
pilau	putrid
pilikia	trouble
pohaku	rock, stone
popoki	cat
pua	flower, blossom
pua'a	pig, pork
puka	hole, door
pupu	shell, hors d'oeuvre
pupule	crazy, insane
tutu	grandmother
tutu kane	grandfather
wahine	female, wife
wai	fresh water
wikiwiki	fast, hurry

Haleakala~House of the Sun

When you reach the overlook atop Haleakala, Maui's 10,023-foot volcano, you will have traveled the only paved road in the world that climbs to that height from sea level in just 40 miles. The views from the summit are spectacular. Off to the southeast, the tops of Hawaii's Mauna Loa and Mauna Kea float in a sea of clouds. As you turn clockwise, other islands and the rest of Maui come into view—unless clouds below blanket them. The air is bracing at this altitude, probably about 30 degrees cooler than in the valley. In winter you may encounter snow, and temperatures sometimes drop below freezing. Bring along a warm jacket.

Haleakala National Park includes the summit and astonishing crater of this dormant volcano, which last erupted about 1790. The crater, low down on the southwest flank, is a vast depression carved out of Haleakala's dome by centuries of erosion. Later volcanic activity partially filled the crater with colorful cones and windswept banks of cinders. It measures 7½ miles long, 2½ miles wide, 21 miles around, 3,000 feet deep, and covers 19 square miles.

According to Hawaiian legend, from the crater rim the demigod Maui, son of Hina, snared the sun. He made it promise to slow down on its path across the sky, giving crops more time to grow, fishermen more time to fish, and his mother's tapa cloth more time to dry. Now the sun is careful to travel slowly, and the great mountain is known as Haleakala—"The House of the Sun."

The total area of Haleakala National Park, 28,665 acres, includes an 8-mile-long strip that extends from the eastern edge of the crater down through Kipahulu Valley to the sea. The lower region of this addition, near the mouth of 'Ohe'o stream, is accessible (see page 38), but the ecologically fragile virgin forest above 3,100 feet, now a biological preserve, is closed to entry.

The Drive to the Top

Before you start the 1½-hour drive from Kahului to the summit, phone 572-7749 for a taped report on current travel information and weather conditions. The message is updated during the day as conditions change. The crater's coloring shows up best in the afternoon, but clouds often roll in after 10 A.M.

Persons with high blood pressure or a heart condition are advised against driving alone, since the rarefied air can cause dizziness.

You climb first through cane fields and then through pineapple spreads into the Kula upland. From the turn-off onto Highway 378, a serpentine route leads up through pastures—and perhaps through a layer of clouds—into rocky wasteland.

Hosmer Grove. Just past the park entry sign, a paved side road leads in about ½ mile to Hosmer Grove, a small campground and picnic area ringed with North American pine, cedar, juniper, and spruce trees, deodar from India, cryptomeria from Japan, and eucalyptus from Australia. Trees are labeled along a short, level nature trail, and a sign at the start of the trail identifies birds commonly seen here. Open daily from 7:30 A.M. to 4 P.M., park headquarters lie at 7,030 feet, a mile past the entrance. Here you can pick up a park map-guide and other material and can get help in planning crater trips. An enclosure near the headquarters building permits a closeup look at Hawaii's state bird, the *nene*.

Some good viewpoints. You can stretch your legs at several points along the 10¼ miles between park headquarters and the top. At 8,000 feet, walk a mile on Halemauu Trail to the crater rim, where you can look across Koolau Gap, down Keanae Valley, and ahead to the trail zigzagging down the crater wall. There's a similar view at 8,800 feet from Leleiwi Overlook, just a 350-yard walk from the road. Here, in late afternoon, you may see the "Spectre of the Brocken"—your shadow against the clouds, encircled by a rainbow.

Just above, a road goes to Kalahaku Overlook, where you'll find some of Haleakala's famous silverswords and exhibits relating to the crater's cones and lava flows. The silversword, a relative of the sunflower, grows from 4 to 20 years as a rounded mass of stiletto-shaped leaves before sending up a flower stalk as tall as 9 feet with 100 or more purplish blossoms. Blooms develop from May through October. The plant flowers only once and then dies—but not before it sends out seeds to start new silverswords. Except for a few plants on the Big Island, this species of silversword is unique to its isolated habitat on Maui. Another variety grows in very wet areas in the West Maui Mountains.

When You Reach the Summit

Two visitor shelters sit atop the mountain: the Haleakala Visitor Center, on the rim at 9,745 feet, and Puu Ulaula Visitor Center, ½ mile farther up on Red Hill, the actual summit.

Exhibits at Haleakala Visitor Center explain the crater's features and formation. From here you look down on slopes of cinder blown by the easterly trade winds against the rocks of the original rim. Koolau Gap on the north and Kaupo Gap on the south cut the rim. Beyond Koolau, Hanakauhi's peak often protrudes from a blanket of clouds. On the opposite rim, Haleakala peak stands out like a fortress above Kaupo Gap.

Symmetrical cones of varied hues look like small mounds of sand in the crater, but each is several hundred feet high. The largest, Puu O Maui, rises 615 feet from the crater floor. In remarkable contrast to the naked summit slopes are the meadow and stand of trees at the crater's east end, 7½ miles away, where the annual rainfall is 250 inches.

From Haleakala Visitor Center, a trail climbs 380 yards to White Hill, past ruins of stone wind barriers built by the Hawaiians for sleeping enclosures. The hill is formed of andesite, lighter in color than most Hawaiian lava. Walk a short distance down Sliding Sands Trail to get the feel of the crater; but remember, at this altitude it's an exhausting climb back up.

From Puu Ulaula Visitor Center at the summit, you have a 360-degree panorama of the crater and, on a clear day, of west Maui and the islands of Hawaii, Kahoolawe, Lanai, Molokai, and Oahu.

On pages 32–33 you'll find information on viewing the spectacular sunrises—or sunsets—from high atop Haleakala's summit. You'll also learn how to get down into the crater for a few hours' hike or horseback ride, or for an overnight camping trip.

Science City. You can continue for a mile beyond the park, along the dead-end Skyline Drive through "Science City," with its domes and antennae for communications and space study. Although the facilities are not open to the public, you'll be rewarded with a precipitous view down to the Lualailua Hills and the south coast desert.

Among the occupants of the 18-acre science site are the Air Force, University of Hawaii Institute of Geophysics, and North American Air Defense Command.

Wildlife. On Haleakala's windward side the bare, moonlike setting gives way to lush forest plantings, home to most of the island's wildlife. Around 'Ohe'o Gulch you'll find doves, cardinals, Japanese white-eyes, mynahs, and ring-necked pheasants. Sea birds such as the frigate bird and the white-capped noddy tern can sometimes be seen wheeling above the mountain slopes.

You may see the weasel-like mongoose (a native of India introduced here in 1883) along the road. Wild goats roam the mountain's high ridges and feral pigs root through the forests.

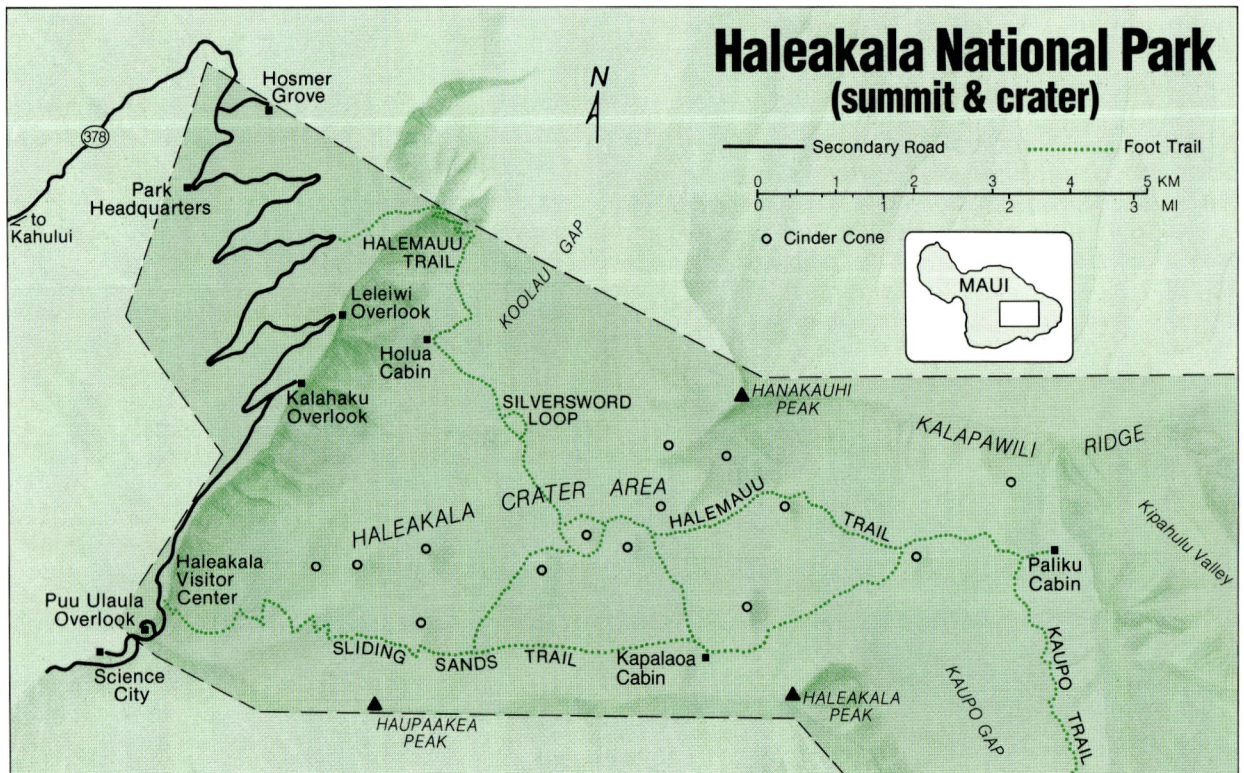

Haleakala National Park (summit & crater)

Haleakala, Maui's "House of the Sun,"
reveals its quiet, eerie interior.

Visiting the Crater~ An Experience to Remember

A Valley Isle vacation isn't complete without a visit to Haleakala National Park. You can hike or ride into the moon-like crater, camp in its depths, visit the waterfalls on its windward side, or greet the sun from its rim.

Watching the sunrise

Few if any places in the world can match the sunrise view from atop Haleakala. Though it requires getting up at a wide-yawning hour (3 A.M. departure for the 2 to 2½-hour drive from West Maui resort areas), the trip is an adventure not soon to be forgotten.

You'll know that the long, winding drive through the dark was worth it when you look eastward to see the Big Island start to take shape as the murkiness of night gradually gives way to the first faint signs of daylight.

When the huge, round, golden star of the show makes its dramatic appear-

Sunrise atop Haleakala

ance through the clouds, you'll realize why Haleakala means "House of the Sun" in Hawaiian.

Dress warmly for the predawn pilgrimage. Atop windy Haleakala, it can get down to freezing at night, and in winter months the wind chill factor can be extreme, day or night. Daytime temperatures are pleasant but about 30° cooler than at beach areas.

Park entrance fees are $3 per car or $1 for bus riders and cyclists over 16. Two shelters offer some protection from the chill: the Haleakala Visitor Center (open most days), on the rim at 9,745 feet, and Puu Ulaula observation point (no rest rooms), 1 mile beyond at the summit. But for unobscured views and picture taking, you'll want to find a good outdoor perch.

Pack a picnic breakfast and hot drinks to enjoy with the view (there's no food in the park)—and plan to stay a while. It's slow going on the curving road as visitors make their way out of the park after sunrise.

For a taped report (updated daily) on weather conditions and sunrise times, call 572-7749. Even if clouds are forecast, you could find you're above them at the summit.

From Kahului, go southeast on Highway 37 about 10 miles to Pukalani, then turn east onto State 377. In about 6 miles, turn east again onto State 378, the curvy road leading to park headquarters (12 miles) and the summit (10 miles beyond). Be sure your car has a full tank—no gas is available in the park.

Prefer sunsets? If early rising just isn't for you, climbing Haleakala later in the day to view the sunset is a good alternative. The view toward West Maui and Lanai, and the colors of sea and sky, are truly spectacular.

Into the crater's depths

To truly claim you saw Haleakala crater, you should go down inside. The Park Service maintains 32 miles of well-marked trails and three rustic cabins (as discussed and page 55).

Hiking trails. Two main trails, Halemauu and Sliding Sands, lead down into and across the crater. They meet near Paliku Cabin at the east end. Sliding Sands Trail takes you about 6 miles down along the south face to Kapalaoa Cabin and then northeast 4 miles to Paliku Cabin. On Halemauu Trail, you descend the west wall to Holua Cabin, a distance of 4 miles, and then go 6 miles farther along the center of the sloping crater floor. Short trails connect the two routes.

In half a day, you can make a round trip on Halemauu Trail as far as Holua Cabin. For a long day's hike (12 miles) or horseback ride, go down Sliding Sands Trail (avoid this steep trail as a way out), cross the floor on Ka Moa O Pele Trail, and climb out on Halemauu Trail—but unless you're willing to hike extra miles up the road, drive two cars to the park and leave one at the start of each trail. For a good overnight trip with no car problem, take Halemauu Trail all the way to Kapalaoa Cabin one day and return the next. You'll cover about 8 miles each way.

Kaupo Trail is used mostly as a crater exit. From the park boundary, it crosses private ranchland on a steep jeep road to reach Highway 31. The distance from Paliku to the highway is about 9 miles.

Crater-explorers should carry water for trail use (cabins have a limited water supply), a light raincoat, sun hat, suntan lotion, chapstick, and a light jacket or sweater. Be sure you have a good pair of hiking shoes, well broken in. And—perhaps most important of all—make sure you are in good physical condition for hiking.

What you'll find. Down in the weird environment of the crater, you'll see sandalwood trees; lichens, or Hawaiian Snow, the first plant to appear after a lava flow in higher altitudes; mountain *pili*, distinct from the lowland variety once used for grass houses; and volcanic dikes, remnants of an ancient divide that separated the heads of Keanae and Kaupo valleys.

North of Kapalaoa Cabin is Bubble Cave, formed when molten lava was forced up by gases; the lava stayed in that position until it cooled and later was opened when part of the top collapsed.

At rainy Paliku, large native trees (*ohia lehua, kolea, olapa*), tall grass, and ferns create a haven in the barren waste. Here you occasionally will see the *nene* (Hawaii's state bird).

On Halemauu Trail you pass Bottomless Pit, an old spatter vent, which looks like a 10-foot-wide well. The bottom is 65 feet down—so keep away from the crumbly edges. Nearby are Pele's Paint Pot, a colorful pass between cinder cones, and, on a cross trail, Pele's Pig Pen, a half-buried spatter vent. Near Holua Cabin you'll find the Silversword Loop Trail.

Kapalaoa, Paliku, and Holua cabins. Each cabin accommodates 12 persons. Cabins have bunks, firewood cookstoves, and eating and cooking utensils. Cabin users must bring their own sleeping bags and light source. Reservations for cabins must be made by mail at least 90 days in advance and are limited to three nights per month with only two consecutive nights in any one cabin. Write Haleakala National Park, Box 369, Makawao, HI 96768, giving your social security number, the exact days, the number in your party, and which cabins you wish to use. Because of their popularity, cabin assignments are decided by lottery.

Campsites. Holua and Paliku also have camping sites. A permit is required (obtainable at park headquarters); length-of-stay limits are the same as for the cabins. No open fires are allowed, and campers should have a warm sleeping bag and tent with rain fly for cold or wet weather. Camping groups are limited to 15 people.

Guided horseback rides. Trail rides vary from a 2-hour trip to all-day excursions. For information, see page 53.

Highway to Hana

Isolated on the eastern tip of Maui not so much by distance as by time and terrain, Hana is an island within an island. The Maui visitor who leaves without dropping in on "heavenly Hana" misses an opportunity to see a fragment of old Hawaii at its scenic best.

More than the little settlement usually known as Hana town, the Hana area ranges far up Haleakala's lush eastern slopes and stretches for miles along the dramatic shoreline.

Ask any of Hana's 700 residents why the area hasn't changed over the years and many will shrug, then smile and blame it on the road—a 62-mile squiggle that state officials have the nerve (or sense of humor) to call the Hana Highway. Certainly one of the most cantankerous stretches of pavement in the islands, it is also one of the most spectacular.

Threading a cautious route above a rocky, wave-pounded coastline, it passes through some of the island's wildest tropical forests. Trails beckon everywhere, leading beneath the jungle canopy into deep rain forests where green light softens the vibrant blooms of ginger and orchids.

Rain is a way of life here. There are 54 bridges on the road to Hana, and at every turn another stream cascades over rocks or plunges into quiet pools that beg for a quick swim.

Close to town, the forest gives way to agriculture: rolling acres of green pasture for cattle, small plantations specializing in papaya and kiwi fruit, commercial nurseries growing cut flowers for export to the mainland. Youngsters sell fruit, flower leis, and shells at roadside stands.

Tucked around the eastern coast's only safe harbor, Hana town is a center for working ranches and farms, complete with general store, gas station, museum, post office, and old church. You make your own entertainment here; you'll find no high-rise hotels, no designer boutiques, no fast-food franchises. There isn't even a stoplight.

Along the Road

You can drive the Hana Highway from Kahului to Hana town in about 2½ hours, but you should allow more time to enjoy the magnificent scenery, perhaps stop for a picnic, swim in a freshwater pool, or just relax a while in one of the pleasant wayside parks along the route.

Your trip begins on a fast, broad highway through cane fields. Just before you reach Lower Paia, you'll find H. A. Baldwin Park, a popular camping, swimming, and surfing spot. Next to it, Rin Zai Zen Buddhist Mission is notable for its graveyard with Okinawan-style family mausoleums resembling miniature houses. The old plantation town of Lower Paia has the look of the Old West, with many restored store fronts, restaurants, and shops. Right in town is handsome Manto Kuji Soto Buddhist Temple. The graveyard, above a sandy cove, has markers carved with Japanese characters.

This highway passes Hookipa Beach Park, where swimming is dangerous but surfers brave some fairly large waves. Championship competition in windsurfing, which in recent years has become one of Maui's most popular water sports, is held here annually.

About 20 miles from Kahului is Twin Falls, an easy-to-reach swimming hole fed by the divided water-course of a mountain stream. Just follow the sign at the start of a short trail 1¾ miles beyond Kakipi Gulch.

By now your road hangs on ferny, pandanus-laden cliffs that drop off to the pounding surf. It twists in and out of gulches, many with sparkling waterfalls. The roadsides are a jungle of breadfruit, koa, *kukui*, *'ohi'a*, and paperbark trees, groves of bamboo, tangled *hau* and guava, giant *a'pe* leaves, wild ginger, and even some rubber trees.

The road follows sections of open ditch—part of the system that takes water from these wet slopes to central Maui's farming areas. The few villages are merely a sprinkling of houses and a general store; occasionally you'll spot old schools and churches. Just downhill from the highway at Huelo, shortly before you come to Kailua settlement, is Kualauapueo Church, built of stone in 1853.

Since the narrow road bridges streams and waterfalls in almost every gulch, you'll often be tempted to stop and look at roadside plantings or admire a distant view. (In any case, if traffic is stacked up behind you, it's a good idea to find a safe place and pull over until it passes.) It's not always easy, though, to find a safe place to pull off the winding road. But three wayside parks within a few miles of one another are inviting:

Kaumahina State Park. About 25 miles from Kahului, a shady park sits atop a cliff overlooking Honomanu Gulch and the Keanae Peninsula just beyond. Far below you can see Honomanu Bay's black sand beach, where natives fish and swim. Picnic tables and pavilions are spread over the neatly landscaped slopes.

Keanae Valley Lookout. A great two-way view awaits you at the lookout—down over Wailua to the sea,

*Many more than seven pools tumble into each other
before finally spilling into the sea at 'Ohe'o Gulch.*

which breaks against Keanae Peninsula in the distance, and up through Keanae Valley to Koolau Gap.

Puaakaa State Park. Between the Wailua and Nahiku turnoffs lies a small park. Manicured paths lead to picnic tables and a cool pond where you can swim through a skin-tingling waterfall.

Wayside Villages

From several high points along the road, you look down on small, quiet villages. The little clusters of houses, church steeples, banana groves, and taro patches resemble South Seas scenes.

Keanae. Take the side road down onto Keanae Peninsula, past the pebbly cove where villagers launch their skiffs. You may see someone pounding taro in the yards of the old wooden houses. Keanae's refurbished coral stone church is more than 100 years old. Picnic under coconut palms or along the rocky black lava shore; the jagged rocks glisten from their constant washing. On a clear day, Haleakala looms up to the south.

Keanae Arboretum, above the peninsula, is planted with native Hawaiian and other plants, including 60

varieties of wetland taro growing on reconstructed old taro patches.

Wailua. The spur road down to Wailua village passes churches and houses fronted with rows of ti and crotons and ends above a narrow cove at the mouth of the stream. Here villagers put out in fishing boats and children body-surf with homemade boards in the late afternoon while their elders relax on the porches.

Quaint St. Gabriel's Church, with its painted trim of red hearts, is known as the Miracle Church. It is said that in 1860, when its builders set out to dive for coral and sand, they found these building materials heaped on shore by the waves. Some of the church's graveyard markers have photographs, and most are decorated, usually with artificial flowers in jars of water.

Take the road inland past Wailua's other row of houses for a close look at the taro and bananas grown for Maui and Honolulu markets. The geometrically terraced plots, set in a gently rising valley guarded by mountain walls, are as neat as a memorial park. Irrigation water trickles downhill from one patch to another in the old Hawaiian manner.

Nahiku. A 3-mile spur road takes you down through Nahiku village, now mostly covered by forest. You pass

*The quiet beauty of Keanae Peninsula's taro fields
evokes the Hawaii of bygone years.*

a few scattered houses, a school, and two churches, ending at the landing used at the turn of the century to unload equipment for building irrigation tunnels through the mountains. Trees here have been left from Nahiku's rubber plantation of more than 80 years ago. You can try out two good swimming holes: one reached by a path from the turnaround at the landing, the other about 400 feet from the wooden bridge and on the right after you pass the churches.

The road from Nahiku to Hana crosses much grazing land. Ulaino Road turnoff leads 1½ miles down to the Pacific Tropical Botanical Garden's Kahuna site. Their ethnobotanical collections flank a large Hawaiian temple. Guided tours are offered on Tuesday by appointment; call Francis Lono at 248-8279. Hana Airport is reached by a turnoff just before you get to a sign directing you to Waianapanapa State Park.

Waianapanapa State Park

Three miles from Hana town, a side road leads to Waianapanapa State Park. Here, a footpath through lush tropical plantings takes you to Waianapanapa and Waiomao caves, two lava tubes near the sea that are filled with water and said to be connected. Waianapanapa Cave has a much-told legend: a Hawaiian princess, escaping from a jealous husband, hid in the underground cavern but, after being discovered by the husband, was slain. The slaying occurred in April, and Hawaiians tell you that the water still runs red with her blood each spring.

Certainly Waianapanapa Cave is an eerie place to swim, but some daring souls take a flashlight and brave the cold water. It's possible to swim underwater, past a point where the roof arches down, into another chamber; there a ledge is said to be the spot where the princess hid.

Out on a point, you'll see a natural rock arch and blowhole; on the grassy ledge where the sea gurgles beneath your feet, three old burial grounds are still in use. Below, Honokalani black sand beach fringes Pailoa Bay. Here you can scout for beach glass or swim when the bay is calm.

The trail to the south of the black sand beach follows the jagged lava coastline to Hana for about 3 miles. Now used primarily by fishers, the trail, called the King's Highway, was part of the original ancient highway built around east Maui by Chief Piilani before his death about 1527. Smooth steppingstones set into the rough lava and cinders have been washed away in places by high surf. Walking time to Hana town is about 1½ to 2 hours.

The park has inexpensive, furnished cabins available by reservation (see page 55).

Hana Town

Quiet Hana town is inhabited mostly by native Hawaiians, though more and more former mainlanders now make their home here. The taro patches, banana clumps, and bits of stone terraces in the nearby gulches provide evidence of the Polynesians who once had a large settlement here. Subsequent sugar, pineapple, and rubber tree plantations were not very successful and finally sold. Since 1944, the fields have been gradually converted to grazing land for several thousand white-faced Hereford beef cattle.

Helani Gardens, a 70-acre commercial nursery, offers 5½ landscaped acres of tropical gardens with picnic areas. Open daily, there is a small admission charge.

Lunch at the quiet and charming Hotel Hana Maui is a pleasant experience and offers the day-trip visitor a welcome break after the winding drive from Kahului. The hotel, located just up from Hana Bay, has lovely tropical plantings in extensive gardens.

A road heads up Lyons Hill (near the hotel) to a cinder cone where a stone cross on a torch-lit platform serves as a memorial to Paul Fagan, who founded the ranch and hotel. There's a nice view down over the rolling hills to Hana Bay.

One of the few modern touches for miles around is Hana's compact shopping center. But still standing is the Hasegawa General Store, subject of the long-popular song of the same name. Look in here for a T-shirt proclaiming "I survived the Hana Highway."

You can inspect a fascinating Buddhist temple, part missionary and part Oriental in style. Sunday

---

It's a long, tortuously slow drive to Hana from any of Maui's resort areas. And yet an increasing number of visitors are taking the challenge. You can leave the driving to someone else by taking a minibus tour (see page 42). Companies offer hotel pick-up and delivery. While the best way to explore all of the beautiful Hana coast is to spend a few nights, if you must do it in a day, here's help.

Driving tips

Stamina is a factor and the main reason we suggest day-trippers turn around at Hana's secluded Hamoa Beach. To Hamoa, *minimum* round-trip driving time from Lahaina would be 6 hours. If you *must* see the Seven Pools ('Ohe'o Gulch), figure at least 7 to 8 hours of driving. Rent a compact car with automatic transmission; it will handle narrow curves best. Carry a windbreaker along with your bathing suit; rain showers and steady trade winds—welcome on most warm days—can be a chilly combination.

Start early. At 6 A.M. you'll miss morning commute traffic from Lahaina and be in Kahului or Lower Paia for breakfast. Phone Picnics (579-8021) by 3:30 P.M. the day before and they will have lunch packed and waiting for you at their Lower Paia sandwich shop by

Hana for a Day: Here's How

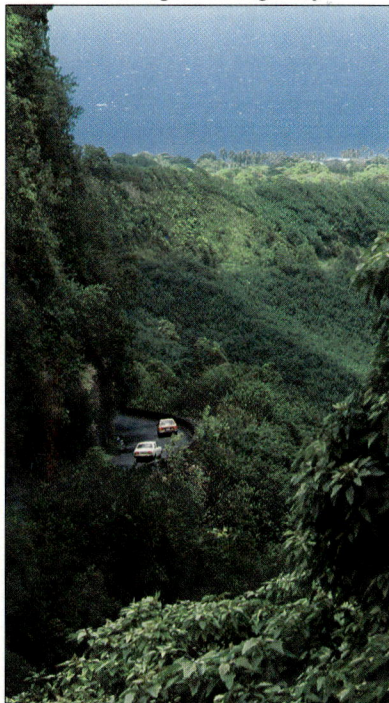
Cliff-hung Hana Highway

7:30 A.M. (Or you can enjoy a buffet lunch when you reach Hotel Hana Maui.) Leave town before 8 A.M. and you'll be well ahead of most tourist traffic, including fast-driving, road-hugging tour vans. If you don't dawdle, you should be in Hana before lunch.

Timing your stay

If you are pushing on to 'Ohe'o Gulch, take a quick break at Hana's small museum, then continue on (with a stop at Wailua Falls 6 miles beyond town) to the park. Stretch your legs on one of the hiking trails, then spread your picnic mat on grassy oceanside bluffs at the mouth of the stream. After a quick dip in the lower pools, start back; leave much after 2 P.M. and you'll be one of a parade of returning cars for a long 4 hours of driving.

If Hana is your destination, work up an appetite by walking through town. Waianapanapa State Park offers good picnicking and oceanside strolling; if it's raining, try sheltered pavilions at Helani Gardens or Hana Bay, then have an ice cream at Tutu's or Hasegawa General Store before heading back. Leave Hana before 3 P.M. to stay ahead of the bulk of the return traffic and you'll be back in Lahaina in time for dinner.

*Misting streamers of Wailua Falls
plunge past couple in rain-forest clearing
at roadside overlook.*

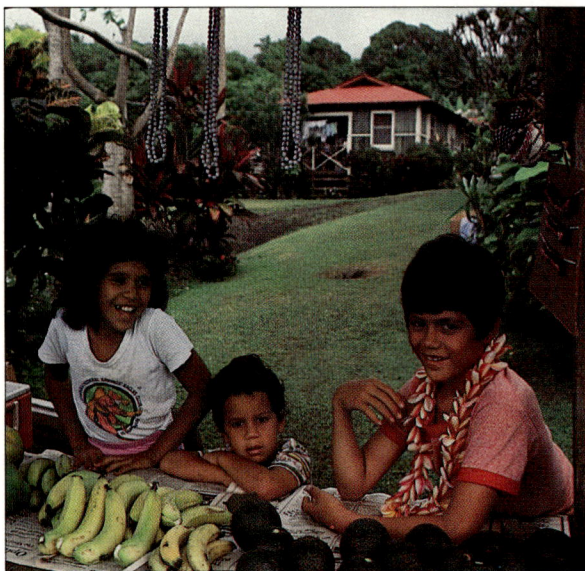

*Roadside entrepreneurs sell fruit, flowers,
and shells in front of their red-roofed house.*

services are still conducted in both Hawaiian and English at century-old Wananalua Church, built by hand of lava rock (some of which came from a *heiau*, temple) over a 20-year period. The nearby Catholic church is also impressive.

Near the turnoff to Hana Bay lies Hale Waiwai O Hana Museum, built to harmonize with the refurbished, century-old former courthouse, just a few steps away. Inside the charming museum are collections of photos and artifacts that chronicle Hana's past.

Kauiki Head, a fortresslike cliff, guards Hana Bay. Here armies of Kamehameha and the king of Maui tangled with slingshots. You can walk down the south side of Kauiki Head to an old cemetery and a red cinder beach, popularly known as Red Sands Beach.

At the foot of Keawa Street, on the bay, is a place known locally as Punahoa. Here, many little springs of very cold fresh water gush out of the sand when the tide is low. You can feel them in the water even at high tide if your foot happens to land on one. Old stories tell of Hawaiians diving down with small-necked calabashes and filling them upside-down with fresh water.

From Hana pier, you can walk along the base of the cliff to a plaque that marks the birthplace of Kamehameha's favorite wife, Kaahumanu, in a cave above.

Hana to Kipahulu

Beyond Hana, Highway 31 continues for 10 miles to Kipahulu, in Haleakala National Park. Near Hana, a side road loops down to Hamoa Beach. (You can use the beach, but facilities are for Hotel Hana Maui guests only. Currents can be treacherous; it's best to stay close to shore.) At the Hana end of the loop, you pass Pele's Hill (Ka Iwi O Pele), where the fire goddess is said to have left her bones when she finished her Maui work and assumed a new body to go to the Big Island.

Where the road turns into Wailua Gulch, two impressive waterfalls topple from Haleakala's slopes. A slippery trail leads down through overgrown mango and breadfruit trees to a rocky beach—site of a settlement wiped out by a 1946 tidal wave. The concrete cross standing above the road is a memorial to Helio, a Hawaiian Catholic who converted hundreds to his faith during the 1840s. South of the falls, gnarled *kukui* trees on the mountainside are the remains of a grove.

A few more turns bring you to the "Virgin by the Roadside," a shrine containing an Italian marble statue. Every day the statue is draped with leis, and once a year representatives from all of Hana's Catholic churches make a pilgrimage to the shrine.

At 'Ohe'o Gulch (often called—erroneously—Seven Pools) you're in the national park. Look upstream and downstream from the bridge to see the pools; 24 of them topple into one another and finally flow into the sea. A path descends the south bank to the most

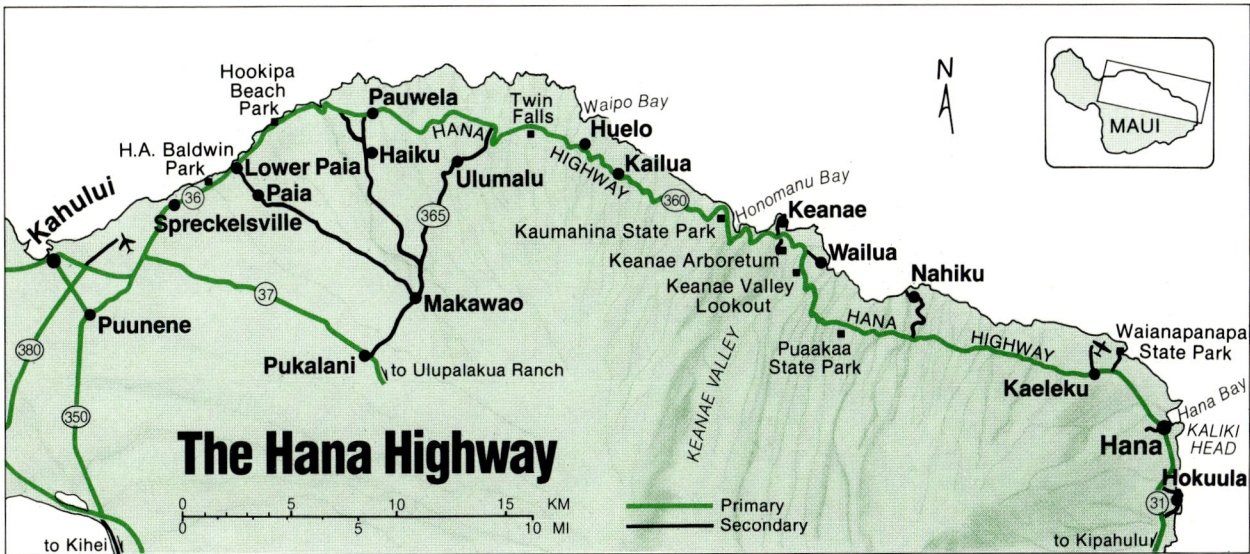

The Hana Highway

accessible swimming and picnicking spots. On the north bank, about 600 yards above the highway is a restored taro farm, funded by the National Park Service and maintained by the Hana Cultural Center. Ranger-led walks and hikes are conducted all year. The pool area tends to get crowded as the day wears on; for your best looks (and most accessible parking), plan to arrive early in the morning.

Paved road ends at Kipahulu Ranch headquarters, near an old mill stack and restored Palapala Hoomau Church, a short walk from the gate on the ocean side of the road. Charles A. Lindbergh, who spent much of his later life in Hana and helped to restore the church, is buried in its clifftop graveyard.

Driving the Southern Coast

Pavement ends a mile beyond the stables in Kipahulu. The scenic but sometimes rugged drive beyond Kipahulu should only be attempted in a four-wheel-drive vehicle. Most rental car contracts ban travel on the road because of frequent washouts.

Kipahulu to Kaupo. A one-lane gravel road links these two towns; you won't see pavement again for about 8 miles. The road hugs the edge of rocky cliffs above the water and dips straight into gulches. If you meet a car, one of you may have to back up to find a safe shoulder.

This country is drier than the Hana area, with open pastures divided by lichen-covered stone walls and abundant *hau* and koa trees. The road edges so close to Lelekea Bay that a heavy sea splashes spray right into your car. You'll see a few outrigger canoes on the rocky beach. A switchback trail visible on the hillside just south is the remains of the old King's Highway.

Kaupo's restored Huialoha Church (1859) and tidy graveyard perch on a grassy peninsula, an inviting place to picnic or camp. Nearby, ruins of a mission school and a heiau on the hill above the road invite exploration. A larger temple, Loaloa (circa 1730), lies at the start of Kaupo Gap Trail, behind the school off the spur road to Kaupo Ranch headquarters.

Whether or not you need to buy something, a stop at Kaupo Store is rewarding. Notice the hitching rail for horses. The store doubles as a post office.

Kaupo to Ulupalakua Ranch. More exciting views of the coastline and distant Hawaii island will greet you as you dip down to the sea at old Nuu Landing, where you'll find village ruins and a salt pond.

The road from here to Ulupalakua is paved and slightly wider. Soon after passing Nuu Landing, you cross a dry river bed, gutted by centuries of flash floods. Walking up to a pool at the head of the gulch, you'll discover caves and petroglyphs.

The gradual climb toward Kanaio carries you through the bizarre landscape of a Hawaiian dryland forest, more pastures, fields of yellow poppies, old lava flows, and cinder cones. About 5 miles farther stands the old Kahikinui ranch house. Nearby, below the road, you'll see the crumbling foundation of Santa Ynez Church.

The blue sea sparkles below as you drive along at 1,500 feet. Offshore you'll see tiny Molokini Island, to some Hawaiians a still-revered home of ancestral spirits, and Kahoolawe, the uninhabited military target island. Along the road are entries to a few grueling jeep trails; two link up with a footpath along the ocean that takes you west to La Perouse Bay.

Between Kanaio and Ulupalakua you look down on the surprisingly fresh-looking lava from Haleakala's last eruption, some 200 years ago. Puu Olai cinder cone, a Makena landmark, juts into the sea.

39

Three islands lie off Maui's west coast. From north to south, you're looking at Molokai, Lanai, and Kahoolawe. Several Maui-based companies offer one-day tours to Molokai and Lanai (see page 42); uninhabited Kahoolawe is off limits for all visitors as it is now used by the U.S. Navy for bombing practice.

Molokai

Though Molokai has long been a popular weekend destination for Honolulu residents, not until recently have other travelers been going out of their way to visit the "Friendly Isle."

Hawaii's fifth largest island, Molokai is a shoe-shaped land mass formed by two volcanic domes. Its western end is rolling tableland; jagged mountains make up the northeast section. Kalaupapa peninsula, the little tongue of land that juts out from the north coast, looks almost like an afterthought.

If you appreciate a quiet place, find fascination in history and old legends, and can understand and identify with people who still value their generations-old way of life above all else, then Molokai offers an experience you will never forget.

You can capture its flavor in one day by visiting the island's most celebrated places—Halawa Valley and the lookouts

Islands in the Distance

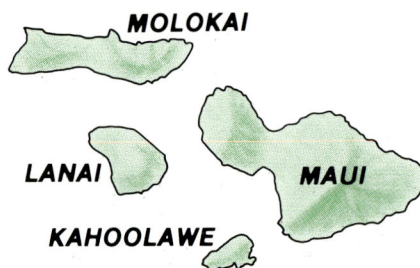

MOLOKAI

LANAI

KAHOOLAWE

MAUI

over Kalaupapa. But a longer stay gives a better look at its spectacular scenery and fascinating historic sites.

Kaunakakai, the first stopping point for most visitors, is a lively little place. People come from all over the island to shop and swap small talk. Barges load and unload their cargoes at the big, busy wharf; fishing boats add to the bustle.

It's less than 30 miles from Kaunakakai to beautiful Halawa Valley—a waterfall-splashed vale. Spectacular Molaula Falls are a pleasant hour's hike

up the valley (take along mosquito repellent). The falls drop from a towering cliff with such force that the surface of the pool below is a mass of bubbles. According to legend, you swim only if the *mo'o* (lizard) is happy. To find out his mood, toss in a ti leaf; if it floats all is well. Even if the leaf sinks, the mountain-cold water is too good to miss.

In another direction, the Kalaupapa overlook offers good views of the tiny peninsula. No roads lead down to the land below; the only ways in or out are by air or on a guided mule ride down the 3-mile zigzag trail.

For almost a century, this was a place of banishment and isolation for sufferers of leprosy. Now that the disease is almost completely under control, those who remain have arrested cases. Though free to leave, they prefer to live out their lives in the place they consider home.

The settlement has several churches, a general store, community hall, bar, and wharf. A monument to the settlement's most famous resident, Father Damien, who devoted his life to relieving the victims' suffering and eventually died from the disease in 1889, stands in the graveyard of St. Philomena, the church he built.

Western Molokai is hilly and picturesque, graced with many Norfolk Island pines. The Sheraton Molokai Hotel offers

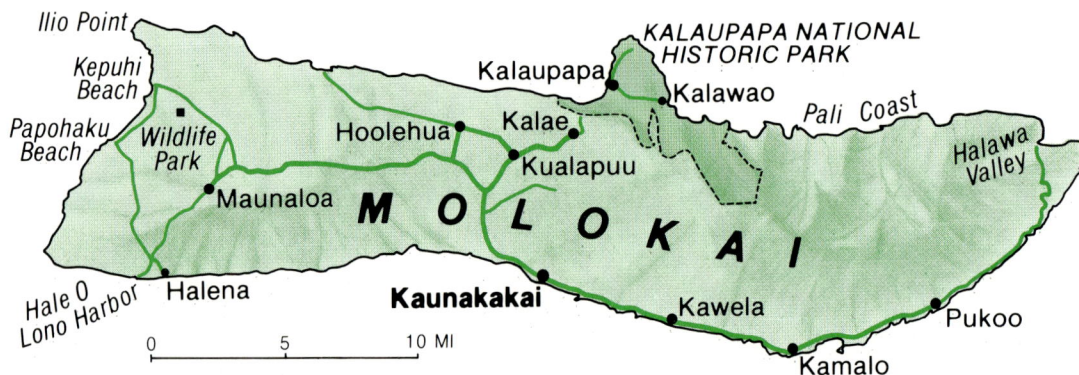

Ilio Point
Kepuhi Beach
Papohaku Beach
Wildlife Park
Maunaloa
Hale O Lono Harbor
Halena
Kaunakakai
Hoolehua
Kalae
Kualapuu
MOLOKAI
Kawela
Kamalo
Kalaupapa
KALAUPAPA NATIONAL HISTORIC PARK
Kalawao
Pali Coast
Halawa Valley
Pukoo

0   5   10 MI

tourists a place to stay. An 18-hole oceanside golf course adds to the resort area's appeal.

Lanai

Long known for delicious pineapples, Lanai has changed little over the years. Just 17 miles long and 13 miles wide, the island is actually an extinct volcano with a single crater. From its southern base, a small, curved ridge rises to an altitude of more than 3,000 feet, sloping down again to the island's northern tip.

Deep gulches cut into its eastern side above a wide coastal plain; on the west, the ridge drops down to a plateau ending in seaside cliffs. Vegetation on the plateau is scrubby, but hillsides on the windward side boast luxuriant growth. All but a few parcels of land are owned by Dole Pineapple.

Excellent swimming and snorkeling, miles of coast made to order for beachcombers, good hunting and fishing all await you on Lanai. If you prefer roughing it to the trappings of tourist resorts, you'll delight in exploring the little-traveled forests, slopes, and desert of this small island.

Many visitors arrive at Manele Bay's small boat harbor on the south coast. To the west lies Hulopoe Bay, with a tree-fringed swimming beach (best on the island but with an abrupt offshore drop-off), rock-rimmed children's pool, and the island's only improved picnic site.

Bluffs along this coast were once submerged, and marine fossils have been found as high as 1,200 feet. Both Manele and Hulopoe are part of the marine life conservation district. Be sure to heed the posted restrictions.

The main and, in fact, only residential area on the island is Lanai City. Situated at 1,600 feet, its climate resembles a California mountain town in summer—comfortably cool days and crisp nights. The hundreds of towering Norfolk Island and Cook Island pine trees around town were planted by the pineapple company.

Here the small Hotel Lanai offers overnight accommodations in a comfortable, white frame, former plantation building. Also in the tidy town is a justly famed bakery that serves breakfast and lunch.

There are no such things as traffic jams in Lanai City and nary a stoplight to be seen—here or anywhere else on the island.

If you have time to explore the island, you can rent a four-wheel-drive vehicle (the best way to get around). Dirt roads crisscross the pineapple fields. Before starting out for offbeat areas, get good directions.

About 7 miles along a dirt road out of Lanai City lies the Garden of the Gods, a varicolored canyon of windswept sand with fantastic lava formations.

A fishing village during the time of Kamehameha the Great and now a national historic landmark, Kaunolu Village (reached by jeep trail) contains a collection of Hawaii's most extensive and best preserved ruins. You'll see remains of a *heiau* (temple), houses, stone shelters, grave markings, and garden sites. All lie scattered across a point above the sea.

Kahoolawe

Looming 7 miles off Maui's southwest coast is the uninhabited isle of Kahoolawe. A barren, windswept land, its only "residents" are a few wild goats who are able to survive on its sparse vegetation and fickle streams.

For over 40 years it's been the target range for naval artillery and bombers. But native Hawaiians are still trying to get it back. In 1981, Kahoolawe became a national historic site—the only one routinely bombed by the government that decided it was worthy of protection.

Fronting Kahoolawe is tiny Molokini, a sunken volcano whose exceptional snorkeling waters can be visited on half-day boat excursions from Maui.

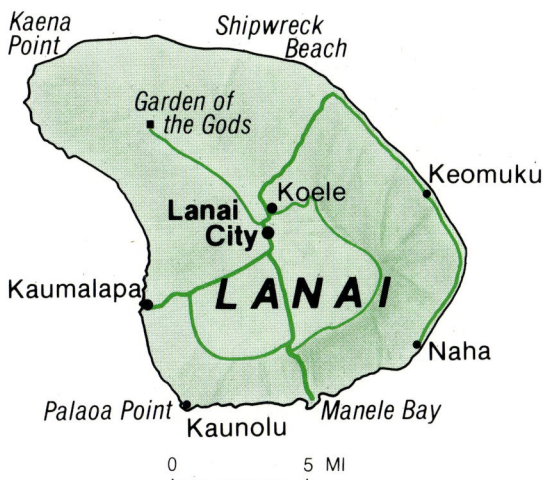

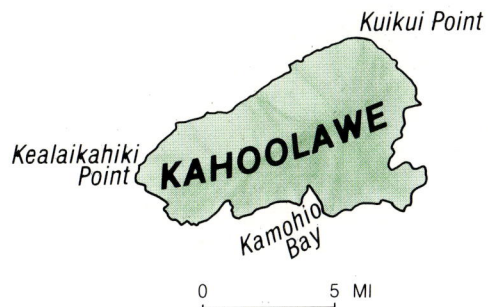

Tours

Viewing the Valley Isle's well-known attractions and hidden wonders on a guided tour is a good way for first-time vacationers to explore Maui. Comfortable cars and vans take you to Haleakala's summit for sunrise or easily negotiate the curling road to Hana; bus tours combine island history and scenery. Or, if you prefer to travel on your own, you can pick up a rental tape for a self-guiding tour.

Listed below are some of the island's major tour operators. Contact them for information on prices and reservations, or check with your hotel's activities desk.

Land Tours

Akamai Tours
P.O. Box 395
Kahului, Maui, HI 96732
871-9551
Air-conditioned minibuses offer four Maui tours and overnight visits to neighboring islands.

Aloha Nui Loa Tours
101 N. Kihei Rd.
Kihei, Maui, HI 96753
879-7044
Full-day Hana excursions, half-day trips to Haleakala Crater, and private tours in air-conditioned vans.

Arthur's Rolls Royce Limousine Service
P.O. Box 11865
Lahaina, Maui, HI 96761
669-5466, (800) 345-4667
Classic limo tours to Hana and Haleakala.

Discover Maui Consultants
P.O. Box 2121
Kahului, Maui, HI 96732
871-6098, (800) 233-MAUI
One-day adventures to Lanai and Molokai plus personalized vacation planning including lei greetings, accommodations, and activities.

Ekahi Tours
205 Pukalani St.
Makawao, Maui, HI 96768
572-9775
In-depth looks at Hana and the Keanae Peninsula.

Grayline-Maui
273 Dairy Rd.
Kahului, Maui, HI 96732
877-5507, (800) 367-2420
Variety of bus tours from one of Maui's largest operators.

Kihele Maui Tours
P.O. Box 983
Wailuku, Maui, HI 96793
871-2555
Maui and other island flightseeing includes ground tours.

No Ka Oi Scenic Tours
P.O. Box 1827
Kahului, Maui, HI 96732
871-9008
Three-day trip along the Hana coastline with buffet lunch at Hotel Hana Maui, half-day tour of West Maui, Haleakala sunrise and sunset trips; air-conditioned vans.

Robert's Hawaii
P.O. Box 1563
Kahului, Maui, HI 96732
871-6226
One of Maui's oldest ground transportation agencies covers Kaanapali, Lahaina, and other areas; tours include day trips to other islands.

Tom Barefoot's Cashback Tours
626 Front St.
Lahaina, Maui, HI 96761
661-8889
Old-line tour and activity center plus off-island adventures.

Trans Hawaiian Maui
845 Palapala Dr.
Kahului, Maui, HI 96732
877-7308, (800) 654-2282
Ground transportation plus island tours.

Rental Tape Tours

Cassette Tours of Maui
West Maui Center
Suite 11
910 Honoapiilani Hwy.
Lahaina, Maui, HI 96761
661-8246
Tapes of historic Lahaina, West Maui, Haleakala/Iao Needle, and Hana.

Hana Cassette Guide
200 Keolalani St.
Pukalani, Maui, HI 96788
572-0550
Hana and Haleakala/Iao Valley tapes.

Flightseeing

Get a bird's-eye view of the Valley Isle from the air. Both helicopters and fixed-wing planes offer flights around the island; early morning and sunset lift-offs are most popular. Most aerial tours originate from the Kahului airport. Rates range from $40 to $200, depending on the length of flight.

You can gaze into the world's largest crater, spin over the island for lunch in Hana, cross the channel to visit neighboring Molokai or Lanai, or spend a day on Oahu or the Big

Helicopter soars over Haleakala crater, giving passengers bird's-eye views of cindery, moonlike landscape.

Island. Stirring music and personal narration add to the air tour's appeal.

The following companies offer tours. For additional information on rates and routes, check with your hotel's activities desk.

Alex Air Helicopters
Kahului, Maui, HI 96732
871-0792
Short West Maui tours and 1½-hour round-the-island flights.

Hawaii Helicopters
P.O. Box 330010
Kahului, Maui, HI 96733
877-3900
West Maui, Hana, and Haleakala plus circle-island tours.

Kenai Helicopters
P.O. Box 685
Puunene, Maui, HI 96784
871-6463
Choose 35-minute island "peeks" or longer tours, some include Molokai; special beach picnics.

Maui Helicopters
P.O. Box 1002
Kihei, Maui, HI 96753
879-1601
Swoop and swirl around Maui and Molokai from Kihei/Wailea; sunset flights also available.

Papillon Helicopters
Kaanapali Hills Heliport
P.O. Box 1690
Lahaina, Maui, HI 96767
669-4884, (800) 367-7095
Explore the island's more remote areas on half-hour to full-day flights, some include champagne picnics; takes off from northwest Maui.

Paragon Air
R.R. 1, Box 767
Kula, Maui, HI 96790
244-3356
Small-plane flights (including trips to Hana); many add ground tours.

Richard's Helicopters
Airport Rd.
Kahului, Maui, HI 96732
871-5993
One-hour flights along Hana Highway and up into the mountains, personal video cassette and tee shirt.

South Sea Helicopters
536 Keolani Pl.
Kahului, Maui, HI 96732
667-7765, (800) 367-2914
Variety of scenic flights around Maui, Molokai, Lanai, or Big Island; hotel transportation available.

Sunshine Helicopters
P.O. Box 1286
Lahaina, Maui, HI 96767
661-3047, 871-0722
Personalized tours to your choice of island sites.

Water Sports

Windsurfer catches breezes along the coast near Paia, one of the world's windsurfing "capitals."

Surfer rides the lip of the wave off Maui's west coast.

Great recreation on Maui doesn't stop on land. Offshore the warm waters of the Pacific Ocean invite you to dive into aquatic adventure. We have included a listing of some of the Valley Isle's watery possibilities. Companies change rapidly; for latest information on specific activities, consult your travel agent, hotel activities desk, or the Maui Visitors Bureau, 172 Alamaha St., Suite 100, Kahului, Maui, HI 96732. One note of caution about water sports: In or out of the water, it's easy to get a bad sunburn; wear a water-resistant sunscreen, available locally.

Boating. Though Maui's heyday as an international port of call has ended, many vessels still set sail every day from the Valley Isle's harbors. Small kayaks, speedy catamarans, large motor cruisers, even square-rigged schooners weigh anchor for 2-hour jaunts along the Maui coastline, leisurely dinner cruises, or full-day trips to neighboring islands; many vessels are available for private charter, too. Food provided depends on the type of trip and ranges from light snacks to hearty lunches and full dinners. Most boats offer whale-watch cruises from November through April, a time when humpback whales migrate to warm Hawaiian waters to breed. Whatever your boating pleasure, reservations are a good idea.

Fishing. Charter fishing boats, based principally at Lahaina and Maalaea, make half to full-day shared and private trips. They provide all gear. No saltwater licenses are required. For spearfishing regulations and freshwater licensing and limits, contact the state Department of Land and Natural Resources, 54 High St., P.O. Box 1049, Wailuku, Maui, HI 96793.

Fishing locations. Channel waters between Maui, Kahoolawe, Lanai, and Molokai are good for trolling or bottom fishing. Spots along much of Maui's shores provide fine shore fishing; among the most promising sites are Kahului Harbor, Paukukalo Beach, Waiehu Beach Park, Waihee Beach Park, the Kulanaokalai-Launiupoko area, Nuu Bay, Seven Pools Park, Waianapanapa State Park, and Hookipa Beach Park.

For spearing octopuses or small fish, try the waters off Lahaina, Makena, the Waiehu-Waihee area, Spreckelsville, and around Hana. Pier fishing is possible in Kahului, Hana, and Maalaea bays.

Jet-skiing and para-sailing. For an unusual water adventure, skim across the water on a jet-ski or soar above the waves while para-sailing. Both are easy—a jet-ski steers like a bicycle; to para-sail you just step into a special harness-like seat, hook up to a towline, and float on air. Para-sail flights start at an offshore floating platform off Lahaina; jet-ski conditions are best off Sugar Beach in Kihei and Hanakaoo Beach Park in Kaanapali.

Scuba diving. Diving lets you explore Maui's underwater world. Local dive shops offer introductory dives for beginners, refresher dives, scuba excursions to neighboring islands, certification courses, and equipment rentals. Experienced divers should bring certification cards for scuba rentals and trips. Some charter boats also offer dive cruises. A non-profit organization compiles information on dive companies and dive sites; write Barbara Brundage, Executive Director, Destination Hawaii, P.O. Box 90295, Honolulu, HI 96735, and include $3 for booklet. Before any dive, always check current water conditions.

Diving spots. Ahihi-Kinau Natural Area Reserve, Hana Beach Park, Hanakaoo Beach Park, Honokowai Beach Park, Honolua and Makuleia bays (protected by Marine Life Conservation District status—good diving, but removal of marine organisms prohibited), Kaehu Beach, Kapalua Beach, Keonenui Beach, McGregor Point, Molokini Crater, Oneloa Beach, Polo Beach, Ulua Beach, Wahikuli State Wayside Park, Waihee Beach Park.

Snorkeling. Clear warm water and abundant sea life make Maui a wonderful place to snorkel. Even complete beginners can successfully don mask and fins; most resorts and excursion boats offer lessons. Rent equipment at resorts, dive shops, or beach rental centers; snorkeling is best before 1 P.M. when the wind picks up. Charter boats cruise to snorkeling sites at Molokini Crater and Hulopoe Bay on Lanai (equipment included).

Snorkeling sites around Maui. Ahihi-Kinau Natural Reserve, Black Rock at the Sheraton on Kaanapali, Honolua Bay, Kapalua Bay, Maluaka Beach, Mokapu Beach, Namulu Bay, Olowalu, Ulua Beach.

Surfing. You'll find some of the best Hawaiian surfing on Maui. Before paddling out, check current water conditions with equipment rental companies (see below or in the Yellow Pages under "Surfboards") or your hotel.

Board surfing. Awalua Beach, H.A. Baldwin Beach, Hamakua Poko Papa, Hanakaoo Beach, Honolua Bay, Hookipa Beach Park, Kahului Harbor, Kalama Beach Park, Lahaina Beach, Launiupoko State Wayside Park, Lower Paia Park, Maalaea Beach, Mokapu Beach, Napili Bay, Olowalu Beach, Popolana Beach, Puamana Beach Park, Ukumehame Beach Park.

Body surfing. D.T. Fleming Beach Park, Hamoa Beach, Hanakaoo Beach, Kamaole I, Kamaole II, Kamaole III, Keawakapu Beach, Kulanaokalai Beach, Makuleia Beach, Mokapu Beach, Polo Beach, Wailea Beach.

Windsurfing. "Windsurfing capital of the world"—that's Maui's claim. Warm water and predictable breezes combine to provide ideal conditions for novice and pro alike. Paia is the acknowledged center for serious sailors, but you'll see the bright sails all around the island. In addition to the places listed below, check at hotel activities desks for advice on the best spots for sailing.

For quick reference, we include some of the following symbols:

🚲 Bicycles

⚓ Boat rentals

⛵ Cruises

🐟 Fishing

⛳ Golf

🚙 Land tours

🤿 Scuba dives

🏊 Snorkeling

🎾 Tennis

🐳 Whale watching

Fishing charters offer anglers good opportunities to bring back the big ones.

Lahaina/ Kaanapali

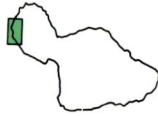

Aerial Sportfishing Charters

P.O. Box 831
Lahaina, Maui, HI 96761
667-9089

Alihilani Yacht Charters

Sunshine Connection
P.O. Box 1286
Lahaina, Maui, HI 96761-1286
661-3047

Aloha Activities

Whalers Village
2560 Kekaa Dr. #G-101
Lahaina, Maui, HI 96761
667-9564

Beach Rental Emporium

888 Wainee St. #104
Lahaina, Maui, HI 96761
667-5857

Everything you need for a day at the beach, including boogie boards, snorkel sets, rafts.

Between The Sheets

P.O. Box 11041
Lahaina, Maui, HI 96761
661-4095

6-passenger maximum.

Blue Chip Charters

P.O. Box 5159
Lahaina, Maui, HI 96761
661-3226, 667-7474 Ext. 3267, 3104

At the Hyatt Regency Maui.

Capt. Nemo's Ocean Emporium

700 Front St.
Lahaina, Maui, HI 96761
661-5555, (800) 367-8088

58-foot catamaran.

Captain Zodiac

P.O. Box 1776
Lahaina, Maui, HI 96767
667-5351

23-foot zodiac-type inflatable rafts.

Central Pacific Divers

780 Front St.
Lahaina, Maui, HI 96761
661-8718

Club Lanai

333 Dairy Rd., Suite 201A
Kahului, Maui, HI 96732
871-1144

Includes use of outrigger canoes, surf ski, floats, fishing poles at private Lanai estate.

Coral See

P.O. Box 218
Lahaina, Maui, HI 96761
661-8600

Glass-bottom boat.

Dive Maui

Lahaina Market Place
Lahainaluna Rd.
Lahaina, Maui, HI 96761
667-2080

Three six-passenger boat trips from Lahaina and Maalaea.

The Duck Jibe

1036 Limahana Pl., Suite 2-I
Lahaina, Maui, HI 96761
667-2104

Windsurfing lessons and rentals at Sands of Kahana, Royal Lahaina Hotel, and Kaanapali Shores.

Snorkeling opens up a colorful, crowded undersea world.

Extended Horizons Diving School

P.O. Box 10785
Lahaina, Maui, HI 96761
667-0611

West Maui pick-up, reservations required.

Fantasy Islands

P.O. Box 98
Lahaina, Maui, HI 96761
661-5315

Para-sailing.

Finest Kind & Exact Charters

Lahaina Harbor, Slip 7
P.O. Box 10481
Lahaina, Maui, HI 96761
661-0338

Fishing Charters Lahaina

Lahaina Harbor, Slip 18
P.O. Box 10459
Lahaina, Maui, HI 96761
661-3448, 667-6625, 667-7548

Genesis Yacht Charters

P.O. Box 10697
Lahaina, Maui, HI 96761
667-5667

48-foot luxury ketch.

Hawaiian Reef Divers

129 Lahainaluna Rd.
Lahaina, Maui, HI 96761
667-7647

Hawaiian Sailing Adventures

P.O. Box 302
Lahaina, Maui, HI 96767
667-7511

Trimaran, 6-passenger maximum.

Kaanapali Jet Ski

Kaanapali Beach
P.O. Box 98
Lahaina, Maui, HI 96761
667-7851

On the beach in front of Whalers Village.

Kaanapali Windsurfing School

104 Wahikuli Rd.
Lahaina, Maui, HI 96761
667-1964

On Kaanapali Beach next to Hyatt Regency Maui; group or private windsurfing lessons, rentals.

Kamehameha Sails

577 Luakini St.
Lahaina, Maui, HI 96761
661-4522

Hawaiian-built 40-foot catamaran.

Kiele V

Hyatt Regency Maui Recreation Dept.
200 Nohea Kai Dr.
Lahaina, Maui, HI 96761
667-7474 Ext. 3104

55-foot catamaran.

Lahaina Beach Center

505 Front St.
Lahaina, Maui, HI 96761
661-5762

Windsurfing and surfing lessons; windsurfer, surfboard, boogie board, kayak, snorkeling gear, beach equipment rentals.

Lahaina Charter Boats

Lahaina Harbor, Slip 8
P.O. Box 12
Lahaina, Maui, HI 96767
667-6672

Lahaina Divers

710 Front St.
Lahaina, Maui, HI 96761
667-7496, 661-4505, (800) 367-8047

Lahaina Para-Sail

P.O. Box 10355
Lahaina, Maui, HI 96761
661-4887

12 flights an hour, wind and weather permitting; also water-ski charters.

Lahaina Shores Watersports

Lahaina Market Place
Lahainaluna Rd.
Lahaina, Maui, HI 96761
661-4363

Linnline Marine Charters

Lahaina Harbor, Slip 15
P.O. Box 1151
Lahaina, Maui, HI 96767-1151
661-3256

45-foot cruising sloop, 6-passenger maximum.

Lin Wa Cruises

626 Front St.
P.O. Box 1376
Lahaina, Maui, HI 96761
661-3392

65-foot glass-bottom Chinese junk.

Luckey Strike Charters

P.O. Box 1502
Lahaina, Maui, HI 96761
661-4406

Deep-sea trolling and bottom fishing, one 22-passenger boat.

Mahana Nai'a Adventures

P.O. Box 11323
Lahaina, Maui, HI 96761
667-7636

58-foot catamaran.

Mareva Charters

P.O. Box 10697
Lahaina, Maui, HI 96761
667-7013

38-foot sloop, 6-passenger maximum.

OLE Surfboards

1036 Limahana Pl. #2-D
Lahaina, Maui, HI 96761
661-3459

Surfboard and boogie board rentals.

Pacific Jet Ski Rentals

Lahaina Trade Center
1000 Limahana Pl., #D
Lahaina, Maui, HI 96761
667-2066

South end of Kaanapali Beach, next to Hanakaoo Beach Park.

Para-Sailing Hawaii

P.O. Box 415
Lahaina, Maui, HI 96761
667-2191

Pardner Charters
Lahaina Harbor, Slip 18
19 Kaniau St.
Lahaina, Maui, HI 96761
661-3448

46-foot ketch, 6-passenger maximum.

Scotch Mist Sailing Charters
P.O. Box 845
Lahaina, Maui, HI 96761
661-0386

50-foot sloop, 6-passenger maximum.

Scuba Schools of Maui
Lahaina Trade Center
1000 Limahana Pl., #A
Lahaina, Maui, HI 96761
661-8036

Seabern Yachts
Lahaina Harbor, Slip 64
P.O. Box 1022
Lahaina, Maui, HI 96761
661-8110

42-foot yacht.

Seabird Cruises
120 Dickenson St.
P.O. Box 1553
Lahaina, Maui, HI 96767-1553
661-3643, (800) 442-SAIL

Catamaran fleet.

Sea Sails
Kaanapali Beach
P.O. Box 10758
Lahaina, Maui, HI 96761-0758
661-0927

50-foot catamarans; windsurfing, hobie cat, and scuba lessons; complete equipment rentals.

Trilogy Excursions
180 Lahainaluna Rd.
P.O. Box 1121
Lahaina, Maui, HI 96767
661-4743, (800) 874-2666

50-foot trimaran and 40-foot catamaran sail to Lanai.

Tropical Dive & Sail
711 Mill St.
Lahaina, Maui, HI 96761
661-5488

UFO Paracruiser
4435 L. Honoapiilani Rd., Apt. 247
Lahaina, Maui, HI 96761
669-7719

Para-sailing in front of Whalers Village.

West Maui Parasail
P.O. Box 1793
Lahaina, Maui, HI 96767
661-2060

Daily flights (singles and tandems) at Lahaina Harbor, observers welcome.

Windjammer Maui
P.O. Box 218
Lahaina, Maui, HI 96767
667-6834, 661-8600

65-foot 3-masted schooner, 65-foot glass-bottom motorboat, 48-foot motor yacht.

North of Kaanapali

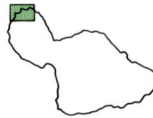

Kapalua Beach Activities
P.O. Box 10056
Lahaina, Maui, HI 96761
669-4664

Catamarans, glass-bottom kayaks; windsurfing lessons; complete equipment rentals.

Southwest Coast

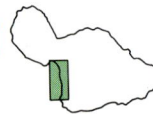

Apple Annie's Deep Sea Fishing Charters
Maalaea Harbor
PCB #426
Maui Mall
Kahului, Maui, HI 96732
871-9521

Aquatic Charters of Maui
132 Kupuna St.
Kihei, Maui, HI 96753
879-0976

Classic Ventures
P.O. Box 1052
Kihei, Maui, HI 96753
242-4076, 879-7986

43-foot cutter, 6-passenger maximum.

The Dive Shop of Kihei
1975 S. Kihei Rd.
Kihei, Maui, HI 96753
879-5172

Excel Fishing Charters
Maalaea Harbor, Slip 61
P.O. Box 146
Makawao, Maui, HI 96768
661-5559

Friendly Charters & Activities
Maalaea Harbor
P.O. Box 245
Kahului, Maui, HI 96732
871-0985

Catamarans.

Hawaiian Watercolors
P.O. Box 616
Kihei, Maui, HI 96753
879-3584

Island Activities
P.O. Box 530
Kihei, Maui, HI 96753
242-7026

43-foot sailboat.

Jammin Jet Skis
101 N. Kihei Rd.
Kihei, Maui, HI 96753
879-1367

On S. Kihei Rd. across from Suda's store.

Lanai Snorkel Cruise & Land Tour
3750 Wailea Alahui #D-2
Wailea, Maui, HI 96753
879-4485

Maui Charter Fishing

P.O. Box 146
Makawao, Maui, HI 96768
877-3333

Maui Classic Charters

Maalaea Harbor, Slip 49 & 51
1993 S. Kihei Rd., Rm. 210
Kihei, Maui, HI 96753
879-2307

46-foot racing catamaran, 60-foot
square-rigged schooner.

Maui-Molokai Sea Cruises

831 Eha St.
Wailuku, Maui, HI 96793
242-8777

Prince Kuhio, motor yacht.

Maui Dive Shop

P.O. Box 1018
Kihei, Maui, HI 96753
879-3388

Locations at Azeka Place and Rainbow
Mall in Kihei, Lahaina Cannery store
opening January 1987.

Maui Sailing & Activity Center

Kealia Beach Plaza
101 N. Kihei Rd.
Kihei, Maui, HI 96753
879-5935

Windsurfing lessons, hobie cat and
windsurf rentals.

Maui Ultimate Tours

P.O. Box 1116
Kihei, Maui, HI 96753
879-8779

Ocean Activities Center

3750 Wailea Alanui D-2
Kihei, Maui, HI 96753
879-4485

Catamarans.

Outer Reef Charters

P.O. Box 343
Kihei, Maui, HI 96753

Introductory dives.

Pacific Whale Foundation

101 N. Kihei Rd., Suite 25
Kihei, Maui, HI 96753
879-8811

Trips led by marine biologists; ticket
proceeds fund humpback whale
research and conservation programs.

Suntan Special

145 N. Kihei Rd.
Kihei, Maui, HI 96753
874-0332

50-foot sailing yacht, 16-passenger
maximum.

Tabree's Ocean Rentals

61 S. Kihei Rd.
Kihei, Maui, HI 96753
879-8779

Snorkel equipment rentals.

White Wings Charters

Maalaea Harbor, Slip 64
572-8457

35-foot trimaran, 6-passenger
maximum.

Kahului/ Wailuku

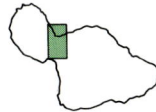

Carol Ann Charters

111 Kahului Beach Rd. #D-223
Kahului, Maui, HI 96732
877-2181

Freedom Maui

55 Kaahumanu Ave.
Kahului, Maui, HI 96732
871-2662

Windsurfing rentals and lessons.

Hawaiian Island Windsurfing

460 Dairy Rd.
Kahului, Maui, HI 96732
871-4981, (800) 231-6958

Windsurfing rentals and lessons,
vacation packages.

Hi-Tech Sailboards

230 Hana Hwy.
Kahului, Maui, HI 96732
877-2111

Windsurfing rentals.

Maui Windsurfari

P.O. Box 330254
Kahului, Maui, HI 96732
874-0338

Daily clinics, complete windsurfing
vacation packages.

Sailboards Maui

201 Dairy Rd.
Kahului, Maui, HI 96732
871-7954

Windsurfing rentals.

Second Wind

111 Hana Hwy.
Kahului, Maui, HI 96732
877-7467

Private windsurfing lessons; surfboard, sailboard, snorkel gear rentals.

Valley Isle Marine Center

625 Haleakala Hwy.
Kahului, Maui, HI 96732
871-8361

Windsurfing West

460 Dairy Rd.
Kahului, Maui, HI 96732
879-8704, (800) 231-6985

Windsurfing clinics, classes.

Upcountry

Paia Beach Center

65 Hana Hwy.
P.O. Box 118
Paia, Maui, HI 96779
579-8000

Private and group windsurfing
lessons; windsurfer, surfboard,
boogie board, and snorkeling
equipment rentals.

Golf

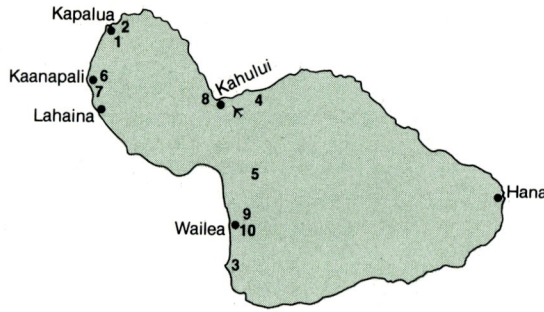

Though Maui's courses range in size and difficulty, it's easy to see why they are such favorites with visitors. Most of them flank the island's western shore, so the Pacific Ocean figures prominently as a water hazard on some holes—not to mention a scenic distraction on many others. And those Maui breezes may also become a factor in your play.

Nine of the ten courses listed below are open to the public at all times; Maui Country Club is open to guests on Monday only. Greens fees for resort courses are similar to resort courses on the mainland; most include cart rentals. Rates for many courses are higher in the winter months.

Kapalua Golf Club

300 Kapalua Dr.
Kapalua, Maui, HI 96761
669-8044

These two impressive courses on Maui's northwest coast are popular with all golfers. Club amenities include two pro shops (rentals, club storage, lessons), driving range, putting green, and adjoining restaurants and bar.

1 The Bay Course

18 holes, par 72

	Yards	Rating
Champ	6,702	73.0
Regular	6,137	69.8
Forward tees	5,232	69.2

Set amid pineapple fields and mountains, the older course at Kapalua boasts two ocean holes and enough scenery to distract even the most avid hacker. The course was designed by Arnold Palmer for high handicappers, but even scratch golfers will find challenges, beginning with the first hole where stiff winds may add difficulties to the uphill par 5. Instead of a halfway house, the Honolua Village general store provides food and drink to go for the back nine.

2 The Village Course

18 holes, par 71

	Yards	Rating
Champ	6,602	70.7
Regular	5,981	68.7
Forward tees	5,134	68.4

Designed by Arnold Palmer and Ed Seay, the lush Village Course climbs more than 600 feet amid stately Cook pines and eucalyptus, offering panoramic views of three islands. Holes 5 and 6 are spectacular; the narrow 130-foot-long 18th green is bordered by a lake and an out-of-bounds. All greens putt true.

3 Makena Golf Course

5415 Makena Ala Nui Rd.
Kihei, Maui, HI 96753
879-3344
18 holes, par 72

	Yards	Rating
Champ	6,798	71.9
Regular	6,262	69.4
Forward tees	5,447	70.1

(Course being re-rated at press time; information may change.)

Located in Makena near the Maui Prince Hotel, this course includes two practice putting greens, driving range, and pro shop (club rentals). Golfers enjoy breathtaking views of both ocean and Haleakala as they confront the narrow fairways and fast greens of the southwestern Maui course, designed by Robert Trent Jones, Jr. Hibiscus bushes serve as 150-yard markers.

4 Maui Country Club

48 Nonohe Pl.
Paia, Maui, HI 96779
877-0616
9 holes, par 74

	Yards	Rating
Regular	6,431	71
Forward tees	5,820	72

Every Monday, one of Maui's oldest courses is open to the public. The relatively flat layout with its view of majestic Haleakala looks deceptively easy; the challenge comes from many trees, long fairways, small greens, and often-gusty winds.

5 Pukalani Country Club

55 Pukalani St.
Pukalani, Maui, HI 96788
572-1314
18 holes, par 72

	Yards	Rating
Regular	6,570	68.9
Forward tees	6,059	68.6

Visit Maui's quiet Upcountry for cooler weather and the only golf course in Hawaii with 19 greens. The course includes a pro shop (club rentals), driving range, and restaurant off the 18th green. Hilly Pukalani's third hole calls for a drive long enough to carry a gulch; designer Bob Baldock provided a less dangerous alternate green. Kikuyu grass makes the fairways slow but gives good lies; wind can be a problem.

Royal Kaanapali Golf Courses

Kaanapali Beach, Maui, HI 96761
661-3691; 667-7111

Jitneys bring players from Kaanapali Beach hotels to face these two championship courses along the Honoapiilani Highway. One pro shop (rentals) serves both courses. Golfers also find putting greens, driving range, club storage and cleaning, and restaurant; lessons are offered by Sunseeker Golf Schools.

6 North Course

18 holes, par 72 (forward tees 73)

	Yards	Rating
Champ	7,179	75
Regular	6,305	70
Forward tees	5,577	71.4

The scenic North Course, designed by Robert Trent Jones, Sr., offers excitement for golfers of varied abilities. Large greens follow hillside contours; their slick surfaces require careful putting. The 18th hole may be the toughest, but the 14th presents a more unusual character with the Pacific Ocean as a water hazard on both sides of the green and a very large sand trap—Kaanapali Beach.

7 South Course

18 holes, par 72

	Yards	Rating
Champ	6,758	72.1
Regular	6,250	69.5
Forward tees	5,658	71.6

In 1977 designer Arthur Jack Snyder transformed the picturesque South links into a course where accuracy counts. Ocean and hillside holes challenge golfers; out-of-bounds on the tough eighth hole places unlucky players in a sugar cane field. On the fourth, golfers gawk when a restored steam train chugs across a turn-of-the-century trestle.

8 Waiehu Municipal Golf Course

Department of Parks and Recreation
County of Maui
1580 Kaahumanu Ave.
Wailuku, Maui, HI 96793
244-5433
18 holes, par 72

	Yards	Rating
Regular	6,367	69.7
Forward tees	5,528	70.8

A challenging mix of beach and mountains awaits players at this public course (driving range, putting green, pro shop with club and cart rentals). The front nine's well-bunkered holes were designed in 1929, the back nine were added 38 years later. The course wanders from the beach up to the slopes of the West Maui Mountains.

Wailea Golf Club

120 Kaukahi St.
Wailea, Maui, HI 96753
879-2966

Maui's southwest coast blesses visitors with exceptional year-round golf weather, generally free from blustery winds. In addition to two championship 18-hole courses designed by Arthur Jack Snyder, the Wailea Golf Club offers putting greens, driving range, and pro shop (equipment rentals, lessons).

9 The Blue Course

18 holes, par 72

	Yards	Rating
Champ	6,743	70.4
Regular	6,327	68.6
Forward tees	5,781	72

Bring your clubs—and play courses favored by champions.

Sitting on the slopes of Haleakala, the Blue Course is good for all levels of golfers. Wide, straight fairways precede narrow, elevated greens with hilly lies. At the second hole, golfers encounter two lakes; the fourth begins with an uphill drive to a dogleg left; and the 16th overlooks Wailea with the islands of Kahoolawe and tiny Molokini offshore.

10 The Orange Course

18 holes, par 72

	Yards	Rating
Champ	6,810	71.9
Regular	6,405	69.1
Forward tees	5,741	71.7

Considered among the top U.S. courses, the spectacular Orange Course combines challenging holes, incredible views, and reminders of old Hawaii. Golfers must contend with holes that dogleg right or left, narrow fairways, elevated tees, and greens that are true but tricky. Unique hazards include ancient stone walls and a natural lava formation on the 18th green.

Tennis

Often called Wimbledon West, Wailea Tennis Center offers players a choice of hard-surface or grass courts.

Tennis buffs will find plenty of courts, many lighted for night play. Public and resort or commercial courts are listed below. Many hotels and condominiums also offer guest facilities. You can rent racquets from tennis center pro shops. Fees are charged for most resort/commercial courts open to the public; public courts are free.

Public Courts

Hana
Hana Ball Park, 2 lighted, 3 grass

Kahului
Community Center, 2 lighted

Kihei
Kalama Park, 2

Lahaina
Civic Center, 2
Malu-ulu-olele Park, 4 lighted

Makawao
Memorial Center, 2

Pukalani
Community Center, 2

Wailuku
Community Center, 7
Maui Community College, 4
(after school hours)
War Memorial, 4

Resort/ Commercial Courts

Kapalua Tennis Garden
100 Kapalua Dr.
Kapalua, Maui, HI
669-5677
10 plexi-pave courts (4 lighted); ball machines, racquet and ball rentals;

lockers, showers, snack bar, lounge. Center offers drill lessons, private lessons, video analysis, round robin doubles

Makena Tennis Club
5415 Makena Alanui Rd.
Kihei, Maui, HI 96753
879-8777
6 plexi-pave courts; new facility with clubhouse, pro shop, snack bar

Maui Marriott Resort/ Tennis Shop
100 Nohea Kai Dr.
Lahaina, Maui, HI 96761
667-1200
5 unlighted courts

Maui Sunset
1032 S. Kihei Rd.
Kihei, Maui, HI 96753
879-0674
2 unlighted courts; free

Napili Kai Beach Club
5900 Honoapiilani Rd.
Lahaina, Maui, HI 96761
669-6271
2 unlighted courts

Royal Lahaina Tennis Ranch
2780 Kekaa Dr.
Lahaina, Maui, HI 96761
661-3611
11 courts (6 lighted, 1 stadium); extra charge after 7 P.M.; instruction available; matches arranged; pro shop (equipment, rentals)

Sheraton Maui Hotel-Tennis Courts
2605 Kaanapali Pkwy.
Lahaina, Maui, HI 96761
661-0031
3 lighted courts

Wailea Tennis Center
131 Wailea Ike Pl.
Wailea, Maui, HI 96753
879-1958
11 hard-surface courts (3 lighted), 3 grass courts, practice half-court, stadium court; pro shop (equipment, rentals, lessons)

Cycling

The best-known bike ride in Hawaii is on Maui—a 38-mile descent from the near-barren summit of Haleakala to the lush fields and sea over 10,000 feet below. Local outfitters offer packaged trips, providing special mountain cruiser bikes, windbreakers, helmets, and gloves.

You follow a cruise leader down the mountain slopes and a support van brings up the rear. Be prepared for chilly morning weather; the summit is usually 30–45° cooler than the beach. Bring along sunglasses and sunscreen.

The 3½ to 4-hour ride (starting at sunrise or midmorning) costs around $80. Included in the price are continental breakfast, brunch or lunch, and transportation to and from your hotel. Make your reservations for this popular excursion before you leave the mainland.

Cruiser Bob's Haleakala Downhill

505 Front St.
Lahaina, Maui, HI 96761
(808) 667-7717, (800) 654-7717

Maui Downhill

333 Dairy Rd., Suite 201 E
Kahului, Maui, HI 96732
(808) 871-2155

Maui Mountain Cruisers

P.O. Box 1356
Makawao, Maui, HI 96768
(808) 572-0195

For around-town pedaling, you can rent bikes by the hour, day, or week; you might want to bring your own 5 or 10-speed for cross-country trips since low-geared bikes are not always available at rental outlets. Check with your airline in advance for regulations and costs of transporting a bicycle.

Riding from Kahului Airport to Hana (52 miles) on Highway 36 uncovers some spectacular scenery. Following a narrow, rough, traffic-filled road, you'll climb some fairly steep hills; the trip can be made in a day, but several good campgrounds (no hotels) are along the route.

Riding north from Lahaina or Kaanapali, you'll discover secluded beaches and lovely panoramas of mountains and ocean. The ride is level and roads are in fairly good condition.

A 2½-mile bikeway parallels the highway from Lahainaluna Road intersection to Lahaina Civic Center (across the highway from Wahikuli State Wayside Park). This area is limited to day trips; bring water and lunch with you.

The new Piilani Highway between Kihei and Wailea is an ideal bike route.

The following shops offer bike rentals (around $10–15 per day); check at hotel activities desks or in the Yellow Pages under "Bicycles" for additional rental locations.

AA Go Go Bikes Hawaii

30B Halawai Dr. #5
Lahaina
661-3063

Cruiser Bob's

505 Front St.
Lahaina
667-7717

Scooter's Bike Rental

1223 Front St.
Lahaina
661-8898

Cycle from Haleakala down to the sea over 10,000 feet below; it's one of Maui's most popular adventures.

Riding

Along mountain trails, across sandy beaches, or down into a volcanic crater—trail rides open up Maui's beautiful backcountry to even novice riders. The following stables offer outings ranging from an hour to overnight. Hourly rates are around $15; overnights (including food and accommodations) start at $125 per person. For detailed information check with the stables or your hotel's activities desk.

Charles Aki, Jr.

c/o Kaupo Store
Kaupo, Maui, HI 96713
248-8209
Overnight trips into Haleakala including cabin or camping equipment and food.

Hotel Hana Maui

P.O. Box 8
Hana, Maui, HI 96713
248-8211
Guided rides take a look at lovely Hana Ranch; nonguests accommodated on a space-available basis.

Kaanapali Kau Lio

P.O. Box 10656
Lahaina, Maui, HI 96761
667-7896

Free pick-up from Kaanapali resorts for guided trail rides through West Maui Mountains; 3-hour rides include refreshments; 5-hour rides add ranch barbecue.

Makena Stables

Makena Rd.
Kihei, Maui, HI 96753
879-0244

Ulupalakua ranch land rides, hourly rentals.

Pony Express Tours

P.O. Box 507
Makawao, Maui, HI 96768
667-2202

Descend from Haleakala's rim to crater floor on 2½-hour narrated ride (lunch included); full-day ride continues to Kapalaoa Cabin; overnight trips; small groups with all levels of experience welcome.

Rainbow Ranch Riding Stables

P.O. Box 10066
Lahaina, Maui, HI 96761
669-4991, 669-4702

Beginners and advanced riders; from West Maui's beaches to its pineapple plantations and forests; sunset and picnic rides; English or Western-style lessons.

Thompson Ranch Riding Stables

R.R. 2 Box 203
Kula, Maui, HI 96790
878-1910

Long-established ranch on Haleakala's western slopes offers family trail rides (small children welcome); sunset, picnic, and overnight rides into Haleakala Crater (all meals included); closed Tuesday.

In the cool Upcountry, riders find plenty of room to roam and unsurpassed views all over the island.

Haleakala National Park is home to the nene, Hawaii's state bird.

Camping

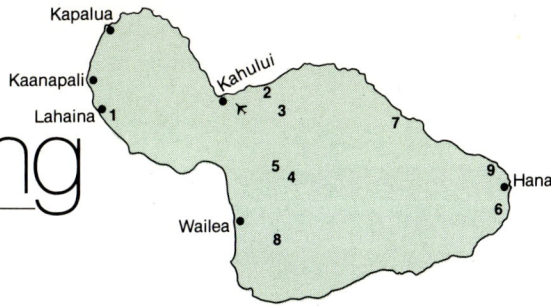

Maui's gentle weather makes camping a year-round pleasure. A sandy beach, a shady forest, or the crater of an ancient volcano—you'll find sites in state and county parks as well as in Haleakala National Park. We also include one private West Maui campground. For specific information (fees, permits, and reservations), contact the organizations listed below.

1 Camp PECUSA

800 Olowalu Village
Lahaina, Maui, HI 96761
(808) 661-4303

Private church camp on a beach 6½ miles south of Lahaina, open to the public with reservations; 6 A-frame cabins (10–42 people); adjacent tent sites.

County Parks

Department of Parks and Recreation
1580 Kaahumanu Ave.
Wailuku, Maui, HI 96793
(808) 244-9018

The county offers camping at two locations; 3-day maximum stay.

2 H. A. Baldwin Park

Swim and surf at this popular wayside park near lower Paia on the Hana Highway; tent space, restrooms, showers.

3 Rainbow Park

Tent camping inland in tiny park between Paia and Makawao; no showers, running water.

Haleakala National Park

U.S. Department of the Interior
P.O. Box 369
Makawao, Maui, HI 96768
(808) 572-9177 information
      572-9306 headquarters

Haleakala's campgrounds reveal some of the park's different environments. All campgrounds are available on a first-come, first-served basis; reservations required for cabins. You'll find water everywhere except 'Ohe'o Gulch.

4 Haleakala Crater

3 cabins (Paliku, Holua, Kapaaloa), 2 primitive campgrounds (pit toilets) with trail access only; permits required; for cabin reservations, write at least 90 days in advance (fees plus firewood charge).

5 Hosmer Grove

Roadside camp just inside park's boundary, ringed with trees; (toilets, fireplaces); ¼-mile nature trail; no permit required.

6 'Ohe'o Gulch

Undeveloped roadside area near the ocean in Kipahulu Valley; (few tables and grills, chemical toilets, no drinking water or firewood); no fees or permits, but stays limited, 50 people capacity.

State Parks

Division of State Parks
54 High St., P.O. Box 1049
Wailuku, Maui, HI 96793
(808) 244-4354

Permits are required at all three no-fee campgrounds; tables, grills, restrooms; 5-day maximum stays.

7 Kaumahina State Park

Forested camp along Hana Highway overlooking the coast; tent camping.

8 Polipoli Spring State Recreation Area

Nights can be cold at the free campsites and 1 low-cost cabin in the Kula Forest Reserve; extensive trail system, sweeping views; four-wheel-drive access.

9 Waianapanapa State Park

12 cabins (reservations required), tent camping; remote and wild volcanic coastline captivates solitude seekers; *hala* forest, legendary cave, small black sand beach; fishing, hiking.

Hiking

Maui's hiking trails offer a way to get close-up looks at the island's natural beauty. Organized hikes head into areas you might not discover on your own.

Though many of the island's hiking opportunities center around Haleakala National Park (see page 32), state parks also provide extensive trail systems. For information, visit the state's Department of Land and Natural Resources (54 High St., Wailuku) or call them at (808) 244-4354.

Other good sources of hiking information include Hawaiian Geographic Society (P.O. Box 1698, Honolulu, HI 96806), Hawaii Trail and Mountain Club (P.O. Box 2238, Honolulu, HI 96814), and Hawaii Sierra Club (P.O. Box 11070, Honolulu, HI 96828). For a free runner's map of Maui, write to Hawaii Safe Running Council (P.O. Box 23169, Honolulu, HI 96812).

Hike Maui

101 N. Kihei Rd.
Kihei, Maui, HI 96753
(808) 879-5270

Fifty naturalist-guided full-day and half-day hikes; hotel transportation, equipment, and picnic lunch included in price.

Charges for custom backpacking trips include equipment, meals, and ground transportation. If you prefer not to camp at night, country inn stays can be arranged.

Resorts

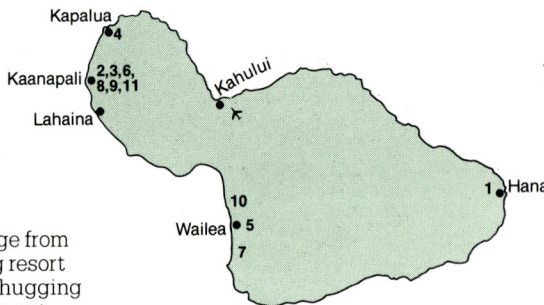

Maui's accommodations range from spectacular beach-sprawling resort complexes to tiny Haleakala-hugging chalets. We have defined a "resort hotel" as a large complex with extensive grounds that offers wide choices in dining, recreation, and entertainment.

To help you plan expenses, we have added the following guide:

$ Inexpensive
$$ Moderate
$$$ Expensive

For quick reference, we include some of the following symbols:

⚓ Boat rentals
⛵ Cruises
🐟 Fishing
⛳ Golf
🤿 Scuba dives
🤿 Snorkeling
🎾 Tennis

1 Hotel Hana Maui

P.O. Box 8
Hana, Maui, HI 96713
(808) 248-8211, (800) 321-HANA
105 rooms and cottages $$$

East Maui's upscale resort; lush grounds, spacious rooms, pool, private beach, 2 restaurants, luau, quiet entertainment; rates include meals.

2 Hyatt Regency Maui

200 Nohea Kai Dr.
Lahaina, Maui, HI 96761
(808) 667-7474, (800) 228-9000
815 rooms $$$

Elegant resort fronts Kaanapali Beach; tropical gardens with waterfalls, spectacular pool, health center, shops, 5 restaurants, disco, entertainment, handicapped rooms.

3 Kaanapali Beach Hotel

2525 Kaanapali Pkwy.
Lahaina, Maui, HI 96761
(808) 661-0011, (800) 227-4700
431 rooms $$–$$$

One of the first multistory resorts along the beach; across from the golf courses, recently refurbished, pool, 3 restaurants, entertainment.

4 Kapalua Bay Hotel & Villas

1 Bay Dr.
Lahaina, Maui, HI 96761
(808) 669-5656, (800) 367-8000
340 rooms and villas $$$

Showplace resort in northwest Maui; 750 landscaped acres with beaches, golf courses, tennis garden, restaurants, and shops, 11 pools; 6 dining rooms (fine buffet lunch), entertainment; handicapped rooms.

5 Maui Inter-Continental Wailea

P.O. Box 779
Kihei, Maui, HI 96753
(808) 879-1922, (800) 367-2960
600 rooms $$$

Beachfront hotel with extensive gardens; 3 pools, spa, Hawaiian arts and crafts activities, 4 restaurants, entertainment, luau, handicapped rooms.

6 Maui Marriott Resort

100 Nohea Kai Dr.
Lahaina, Maui, HI 96761
(808) 667-1200, (800) 228-9290
720 rooms $$–$$$

Luxury hotel extends two wings along Kaanapali Beach; 2 pools, spas, exercise room, shops, 4 restaurants, disco, entertainment.

7 Maui Prince Hotel

5400 Makena Alanui
Kihei, Maui, HI 96753
(808) 874-1111, (800) 321-MAUI
300 rooms $$$

New V-shaped resort on beach in sunny Makena guarantees privacy in posh surroundings; grand courtyard with waterfall and koi ponds, 2 pools, shops, 4 restaurants, entertainment, handicapped rooms.

8 Royal Lahaina Resort

2780 Kekaa Dr.
Lahaina, Maui, HI 96761
(808) 661-3611, (800) 227-4700
514 rooms and cottages $$

South Seas touches in buildings and gardens; recently refurbished rooms, 3 pools, spa, 3 restaurants, entertainment, luau.

9 Sheraton Maui Resort

2605 Kaanapali Pkwy.
Lahaina, Maui, HI 96761
(808) 661-0031, (800) 325-3535
503 rooms $$–$$$

Multilevel hotel abuts Kaanapali Beach's Black Rock; well-landscaped grounds, shops, 2 pools, 2 restaurants (best sunset views from Discovery Room bar) and a poolside snack bar, entertainment, luau.

10 Stouffer's Wailea Beach Resort

3550 Wailea Alanui Dr.
Wailea, Maui, HI 96753
(808) 879-4900, (800) HOTELS-1
347 rooms $$$

Lush tropical gardens with waterfalls and pools; large rooms with lanais, pool, health spa, shops, 3 restaurants, entertainment, luau, handicapped rooms.

11 Westin Maui

2365 Kaanapali Pkwy.
Lahaina, HI 96761
(808) 228-3000
762 rooms $$$

Former Maui Surf to reopen mid-1987 as top-of-the-line resort.

Hotels, Condos & Inns

The following listing of accommodations includes a number of condominiums. Some are indistinguishable from neighboring resort hotels; many offer similar recreational facilities. Others may resemble apartment complexes. Most condominiums include one or more pools and barbecue and laundry facilities. Some condo rates include car rental. The majority are air-conditioned. Not all complexes offer daily (or even weekly) maid service.

Maui 800, a central reservations office, includes listings for many, but not all, of the island's hotels and condomiums; their toll-free number is (800) 367-5224. Other central reservation services include Condominium Rentals Hawaii, (800) 367-5242; First Kihei Realty, (808) 879-4102; Kaanapali Vacation Rentals, (800) 367-8008; Kihei Maui Vacations, (800) 367-8047, Ext. 116; Maui Accommodations, (800) 252-MAUI; The Maui Connection, (800) 628-4776; Maui Diversified Real Estate, (800) 367-8047, Ext. 127; The Maui Network, Ltd., (800) 367-5221; and VIP Village Rentals, (800) 367-5634.

To help you plan expenses, we have added the following guide:

$	Inexpensive
$$	Moderate
$$$	Expensive

Lahaina/ Kaanapali

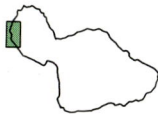

International Colony Club
2750 Kalapu Dr., Kaanapali, Maui, HI 96761; (808) 661-4070. 44 units. $

Kaanapali Alii
50 Nohea Kai Dr., Lahaina, Maui, HI 96761; (800) 642-6284. 264 units; deluxe 1 and 2-bedrooms on Kaanapali Beach; amenities include gym, water sports, sailboat, tennis courts. $$$

Kaanapali Plantation
150 Puukolii Rd., Lahaina, Maui, HI 96761; (808) 661-4446. 62 units. $$

Kaanapali Royal
2560 Kekaa Dr., Lahaina, Maui, HI 96761; (800) 367-7040. 45 units; on golf course. $$

Lahaina Roads Apartments
1403 Front St., Lahaina, Maui, HI 96761; (808) 661-3166. 42 units. $–$$

Lahaina Shores Hotel
475 Front St., Lahaina, Maui, HI 96761; (800) 367-2972. 155 rooms; on the beach. $$

Maui Eldorado Resort Condominium
2661 Kekaa Dr., Lahaina, Maui, HI 96761; (800) 367-2967. 204 units; on the golf course. $$

Maui Islander
660 Wainee St., Lahaina, Maui, HI 96761; (800) 367-5226 . 324 units. $$

Maui Kaanapali Villas
2805 Honoapiilani Hwy., Lahaina, Maui, HI 96761; (800) 367-5124, 367-7040. 200 units; on the beach. $$–$$$

Pioneer Inn
658 Wharf St., Lahaina, Maui, HI 96761; (808) 661-3636. 48 rooms; historic, bayside hotel. $

Puamana
P.O. Box 515, Lahaina, Maui, HI 96767; (800) 362-1521. 228 units; on the beach. $$

Whaler on Kaanapali Beach
2481 Kaanapali Pkwy., Lahaina, Maui, HI 96761; (800) 367-7052. 360 units; on the beach. $$–$$$

North of Kaanapali

Coconut Inn
P.O. Box 10517, Lahaina, Maui, HI 96761; (800) 367-8006. 41 units; continental breakfast. $

Hale Kai Condominium
3691 L. Honoapiilani Rd., Lahaina, Maui, HI 96761; (808) 669-6333. 40 units; on the beach. $

Hale Mahina Beach Resort
3875 L. Honoapiilani Hwy., Lahaina, Maui, HI 96761; (800) 367-8047 Ext. 441. 52 units; on the beach. $$

Hale Maui Apartment Hotel
P.O. Box 516, Lahaina, Maui, HI 96767; (808) 669-6312. 13 units. $

Hale Napili
65 Hui Rd., Napili, Lahaina, Maui, HI 96761; (808) 669-6184. 18 units; on the beach. $–$$

Hale Ono Loa
3823 L. Honoapiilani Rd., Lahaina, Maui, HI 96761; (800) 367-2927. 67 units; on the beach. $–$$

Hololani Condo Resort
4401 L. Honoapiilani Rd., Lahaina, Maui, HI 96761; (800) 367-5032. 63 units; on the beach. $$

Honokeana Cove
5255 L. Honoapiilani Rd., Lahaina, Maui, HI 96761; (808) 669-6441. 38 units; on the beach. $$

Hono Koa Resort
3801 L. Honoapiilani Rd., Lahaina, Maui, HI 96761; (808) 669-0979. 28 units. $–$$

Honokowai Palms
3666 L. Honoapiilani Rd., Lahaina, Maui, HI 96761; (808) 669-6130. 30 units. $

Hoyochi Nikko
3901 L. Honoapiilani Rd., Lahaina, Maui, HI 96761; (808) 669-8343. 18 units; oceanfront. $

Kaanapali Shores Resort
100 Kaanapali Shores Pl., Lahaina, Maui, HI 96761; (800) 367-5124. 463 units; on the beach. $$$

Kahana Beach Resort Condominium
4221 L. Honoapiilani Rd., Lahaina, Maui, HI 96761; (808) 669-8611. 84 units; on the beach. $–$$$

Kahana Reef
4471 L. Honoapiilani Rd., Lahaina, Maui, HI 96761; (808) 669-6491. 88 units; on the beach. $

Kahana Sunset
P.O. Box 10219, Lahaina, Maui, HI 96761; (808) 669-8011. 79 units; on the beach. $$

Kahana Villa
4242 L. Honoapiilani Hwy., Lahaina, Maui, HI 96761; (808) 669-5613. 92 units. $$

Kahana Village
4531 Honoapiilani Rd., Lahaina, Maui, HI 96761; (800) 824-3065. 42 units; on the beach. $$–$$$

Kaleialoha Resort Condominium
3785 L. Honoapiilani Rd., Lahaina, Maui, HI 96761; (800) 222-8688. 67 units; on the beach. $

KulaKane
3741 L. Honoapiilani Rd., P.O. Box
5236, Lahaina, Maui, HI 96761; (800)
367-6088. 42 units; beachfront. $–$$

The Kuleana
3959 L. Honoapiilani Hwy., Lahaina,
Maui, HI 96761; (800) 367-5633.
118 units. $

Lokelani Condominiums
3833 L. Honoapiilani Hwy., Lahaina,
Maui, HI 96761; (800) 367-2976.
38 units; on the beach. $

The Mahana Aston Resorts
110 Kaanapali Shores Pl., Lahaina,
Maui, HI 96761; (800) 367-5124.
150 units; on the beach. $$$

Mahina Surf
4057 L. Honoapiilani Rd., Lahaina,
Maui, HI 96761; (800) 367-6086.
56 units; on the beach. $

Makani Sands
3765 L. Honoapiilani Rd., Lahaina,
Maui, HI 96761; (800) 227-8223.
30 units; on the beach. $

Maui Kai Resort Condominiums
106 Kaanapali Shores Pl., Lahaina,
Maui, HI 96761; (800) 367-5635.
80 units; on the beach, wheelchair
facilities. $$

Maui Sands
3559 L. Honoapiilani Rd., Lahaina,
Maui, HI 96761; (800) 367-5037.
76 units; on the beach. $–$$

The Mauian Hotel
5441 Honoapiilani Rd., Lahaina, Maui,
HI 96761; (800) 367-5034. 44 units;
studios on the beach. $–$$

The Napili Bay
33 Hui Dr., Lahaina, Maui, HI 96761;
(808) 669-6044. 34 units; studios on
the beach. $–$$

Napili Kai Beach Club
5900 Honoapiilani Rd., Lahaina, Maui,
HI 96761; (800) 367-5030. 137 units; on
the beach, restaurant. $$–$$$

Napili Point Resort
5295 Honoapiilani Hwy., Napili, Maui,
HI 96761; (800) 367-5124. 85 units;
on the beach. $$

Napili Shores Resort
5315 Honoapiilani Hwy., Lahaina,
Maui, HI 96761; (800) 367-6046.
107 units; on the beach. $$

Napili Sunset
46 Hui Dr., Lahaina, Maui, HI 96761;
(808) 669-8083. 40 units; on the
beach. $–$$

Napili Surf Beach Resort
50 Napili Pl., Napili Bay, Maui, HI
96761; (808) 669-8002. 54 units; on
the beach. $–$$

Napili Village Apartment Hotel
5425 Honoapiilani Hwy., Lahaina,
Maui, HI 96761; (800) 336-2185.
24 units; along the golf course. $

Noelani Condominium
4095 Honoapiilani Rd., Lahaina, Maui,
HI 96761; (800) 367-6030. 50 units; on
the coast. $$

Nohonani Resort
3723 L. Honoapiilani Hwy., Lahaina,
Maui, HI 96761; (808) 669-8208.
28 units; on the beach. $$

Paki Maui
3615 L. Honoapiilani Hwy., Lahaina,
Maui, HI 96761; (800) 367-6098. 112
units; on the beach. $$

Papakea Beach Resort
3543 Honoapiilani Hwy., Lahaina,
Maui, HI 96761; (800) 367-5637.
364 units; on the beach. $$–$$$

Pohailani Maui Resort
4435 Honoapiilani Rd., Lahaina,
Maui, HI 96761; (800) 367-5221,
367-6092. 27 units. $–$$

Polynesian Shores
3975 Honoapiilani Way, Lahaina,
Maui, HI 96761; (800) 433-MAUI.
52 units; on the beach. $

Royal Kahana Resort
4365 Honoapiilani Hwy., Lahaina,
Maui, HI 96761; (800) 421-0767.
236 units; on the beach. $

Sands of Kahana
4299 Honoapiilani Hwy., Lahaina,
Maui, HI 96761; (800) 367-5124.
196 units; on the beach. $$$

Valley Isle Resort
4327 L. Honoapiilani Rd., Lahaina,
Maui, HI 96761; (800) 367-6092.
119 units; on the beach. $–$$

Southwest Coast

Haleakala Shores Condominium
2619 S. Kihei Rd., Kihei, Maui, HI
96753; (800) 367-8047 Ext. 119.
76 units. $

Hale Hui Kai Condominium
2994 S. Kihei Rd., Kihei, Maui, HI
96753; (808) 879-1219. 40 units; on the
beach. $$

Hale Kai O Kihei
1310 Uluniu Rd., Kihei, Maui, HI
96753; (808) 879-2757. 59 units; on the
beach. $

Hale Kamaole Condominium
2737 S. Kihei Rd., Kihei, Maui, HI
96753; (800) 367-2970. 187 units. $

Hale Pau Hana Resort
2480 S. Kihei Rd., Kihei, Maui, HI
96753; (800) 367-6036. 80 units; on the
beach. $$

Hono Kai Condominium
R.R. 1, Box 389, Wailuku, HI 96793;
(800) 367-6084. 46 units; on the
beach. $

Island Sands Resort Rentals
R.R. 1-B, Box 391, Wailuku, Maui, HI
96793; (800) 244-0848. 84 units. $

Island Surf Condominium
1993 S. Kihei Rd., Kihei, Maui, HI
96753; (800) 367-2954. 80 units. $

Kalama Terrace Condominium
35 Walaka St., Kihei, Maui, HI 96753;
(808) 879-0192. 62 units. $

Kamaole Beach Royale
2385 S. Kihei Rd., P.O. Box 370, Kihei,
Maui, HI 96753; (808) 879-3131. 66
units. $

Kamaole Nalu Resort
2450 S. Kihei Rd., Kihei, Maui, HI
96753; (808) 879-1006. 36 units; on the
beach. $$

Kamaole One Condominium
2230 S. Kihei Rd., Kihei, Maui, HI
96753; (808) 879-4811. 12 units; on the
beach. $$–$$$

Kamaole Sands
2695 S. Kihei Rd., Kihei, Maui, HI
96753; (800) 367-6046. 440 units. $$

Kana'i A Nalu Condominium
R.R. 1, Box 388, Wailuku, Maui, HI
96793; (800) 367-5234. 80 units; on the
beach. $–$$

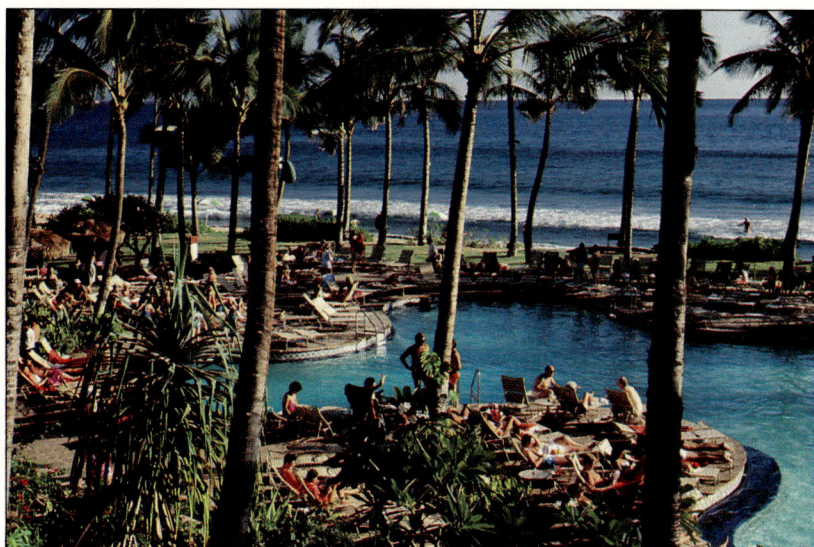

Offering the best of both worlds, dramatic Kaanapali hotel pool lies only a stroll away from the surf.

Kapulanikai Apartments
73 Kapu Pl., Kihei, Maui, HI 96753; (808) 879-1607. 12 units; on the beach. $

Kauhale Makai
938 S. Kihei Rd., Kihei, Maui, HI 96753; (800) 367-5234. 168 units; on the beach. $

Kealia Condominium
191 N. Kihei Rd., Kihei, Maui, HI 96753; (800) 367-5222. 50 units; on the beach. $

Kihei Akahi
2531 S. Kihei Rd., Kihei, Maui, HI 96753; (800) 367-5242. 240 units. $

Kihei Alii Kai
2387 S. Kihei Rd., Kihei, Maui, HI 96753; (808) 879-6770. 138 units. $

Kihei Bay Surf
715 S. Kihei Rd., Kihei, Maui, HI 96753; (808) 879-7650. 118 units. $

Kihei Beach Resort
36 S. Kihei Rd., Kihei, Maui, HI 96753; (800) 367-6034. 54 units; on the beach. $

Kihei Garden Estates
1299 Uluniu Rd., Kihei, Maui, HI 96753; (808) 879-6123. 84 units. $

Kihei Holiday
483 S. Kihei Rd., Kihei, Maui, HI 96753; (800) 367-8047 Ext. 116. 48 units. $$

Kihei Kai Resort
61 N. Kihei Rd., Kihei, Maui, HI 96753; (800) 367-8047 Ext. 248. 24 units; on the beach. $

Kihei Kai-nana
2495 S. Kihei Rd., Kihei, Maui, HI 96753; (808) 879-1430. 180 units. $

Kihei Resort
777 S. Kihei Rd., Kihei, Maui, HI 96753; (800) 367-6006, 367-6007. 64 units. $

Kihei Sands
115 N. Kihei Rd., Kihei, Maui, HI 96753; (808) 879-2624. 30 units; on the beach. $

Kihei Surfside
2936 S. Kihei Rd., Kihei, Maui, HI 96753; (800) 367-5240. 83 units; on the beach. $

Koa Lagoon Condominium Rentals
800 S. Kihei Rd., Kihei, Maui, HI 96753; (800) 367-8030. 42 units; on the beach. $$

Koa Resort
811 S. Kihei Rd., Kihei, Maui, HI 96753; (808) 879-1161. 54 units. $–$$

Laule'a Maui Beach Club
980 S. Kihei Rd., Kihei, Maui, HI 96753; (800) 331-8076. 50 units; on the beach. $$

Lauloa Condo Resort
R.R. 1, Box 383, Wailuku, Maui, HI 96793; (800) 367-8047. Ext. 134. 48 units; on the ocean. $$

Leilani Kai Resort
1226 Uluniu Rd., Kihei, Maui, HI 96753; (808) 879-2606. 8 units; on the beach. $

Leinaala Condominiums
998 S. Kihei Rd., Kihei. For reservations, write to 2145 Wells St., Suite 205, Wailuku, Maui, HI 96793; (800) 367-5234. 24 units; on the beach. $

Lihi Kai Cottages & Apartments
2121 Iliili Rd., Kihei, Maui, HI 96753; (808) 879-2335. 25 units. $

Luana Kai Resort
940 S. Kihei Rd., Kihei, Maui, HI 96753; (808) 879-1268. 114 units; on the beach. $$

Maalaea Banyans Condominiums
R.R. 1, Box 384, Wailuku, Maui, HI 96793; (800) 367-5234. 76 units; on the beach. $

Maalaea Kai Rentals
1709 Hauoli St., Wailuku, Maui, HI 96793; (808) 244-4845. 79 units. $

Maalaea Surf Resort
12 S. Kihei Rd., Kihei, Maui, HI 96753; (800) 423-7953. 26 units; on the beach. $$

Maalaea Yacht Marina Condominiums
R.R. 1, Box 377, Hauoli St., Maalaea, Wailuku, Maui, HI 96793; (808) 242-5997. 45 units; on the beach. $

Makani A Kai
R.R. 1, Box 400, Wailuku, Maui, HI 96793; (800) 367-6084. 24 units; on the beach. $

Makena Surf Condo
96 Makena Rd., Kihei, Maui, HI 96753; (808) 879-1331. 86 units; on the beach. $$$

Mana Kai-Maui Resort
2960 S. Kihei Rd., Kihei, Maui, HI 96753; (800) 525-2025. 140 units; on the beach. $$

Maui Hill
2881 S. Kihei Rd., Kihei, Maui, HI 96753; (800) 367-2363. 140 units. $$

Maui Lu Resort
575 S. Kihei Rd., Kihei, Maui, HI 96753; (800) 367-5244. 170 rooms; on the beach. $$

Maui Parkshore
2653 S. Kihei Rd., Kihei, Maui, HI 96753; (808) 879-1600. 64 units. $

Maui Sunset
1032 S. Kihei Rd., Kihei, Maui, HI 96753; (800) 843-5880. 225 units; on the beach. $$

■ Hotels, Condos & Inns

Maui Vista
2191 S. Kihei Rd., Kihei, Maui, HI
96753; (800) 367-8047 Ext. 330.
280 units. $$

Menehune Shores Condominium
760 S. Kihei Rd., Kihei, Maui, HI
96753; (808) 558-9117 (after 11 A.M.).
154 units; on the beach. $$

Milowai Condominium
Hauoli St., Maalaea, R.R. 1, Box 379,
Wailuku, HI 96793; (800) 367-8047
Ext. 116. 48 units; on the beach. $

Nani Kai Hale
73 N. Kihei Rd., Kihei, Maui, HI 96753;
(800) 367-6032. 46 units; on the
beach. $–$$

Nona Lani Cottages
455 S. Kihei Rd., P.O. Box 655, Kihei,
Maui, HI 96753; (808) 879-2497. 8
cottages; on the beach. $

Polo Beach Club
20 Makena Rd., Makena, Maui, HI
96753; (800) 367-6046. 71 units; on the
beach. $$$

Punahoa Beach Apartments
2142 Iliili Rd., Kihei, Maui, HI 96753;
(808) 879-2720. 15 units; on the
beach. $

Royal Mauian Resort
2430 S. Kihei Rd., Kihei, Maui, HI
96753; (800) 367-8009. 107 units; on
the beach. $$

Shores of Maui
2075 S. Kihei Rd., Kihei, Maui, HI
96753; (800) 367-8002. 50 units. $

Sugar Beach Resort
145 N. Kihei Rd., Kihei, Maui, HI
96753; (800) 367-5242. 216 units; on
the beach. $–$$

Sunseeker Resort
551 S. Kihei Rd., Kihei, Maui, HI
96753; (808) 879-1261. 5 units. $

Wailana Sands Resort
25 Wailana Pl., Kihei, Maui, HI 96753;
(808) 879-2026. 10 units. $

Wailea Ekahi
3300 Wailea Alanui, Wailea, Maui, HI
96753; (800) 367-5246. 298 units; on
the beach. $$

Wailea Ekolu
10 Wailea Ekolu Pl., Wailea, Maui, HI
96753; (800) 367-5246. 148 units. $$

Wailea Elua
3600 Wailea Alanui, Wailea, Maui, HI
96753; (800) 367-5246. 152 units; on
the beach. $$$

Waiohuli Beach Hale
49 Lipoa St., Kihei, Maui, HI 96753;
(808) 879-5396. 52 units; on the
beach. $

Kahului/ Wailuku

Maui Beach Hotel
170 Kaahumanu Ave., Kahului, Maui,
HI 96732; (800) 367-5004. 154 rooms;
on the bay. $

Maui Hukilau
100 W. Kaahumanu Ave., Kahului,
Maui, HI 96732, (800) 367-7000. 89
rooms; on the bay. $

Maui Palms
170 Kaahumanu Ave., Kahului, Maui,
HI 96732; (800) 367-5004. 103 rooms;
on the bay. $

Maui Seaside
100 W. Kaahumanu Ave., Kahului,
Maui, HI 96732; (800) 367-7000. 108
rooms; on the bay. $

Wailuku Grand Hotel
2080 Vineyard St., Wailuku, Maui, HI
96793; (808) 242-8191. 25 rooms. $

Upcountry

Kula Lodge
R.R. 1, Box 475, Kula, Maui, HI 96790;
(808) 878-1535. 5 chalets. $

Silversword Inn
R.R. 1, Box 469, Kula, Maui, HI 96790;
(808) 878-1232. 6 cottages. $

Sugar Cove
320 Paani Pl. #4A, Paia, Maui, HI
96779; (808) 877-2842. 18 units; on the
beach. $$$

Hana

Hana Bay Vacation Rentals
P.O. Box 318, Hana, Maui, HI 96713;
(808) 248-7727. 10 houses. $–$$$

Hana Kai-Maui Resort
P.O. Box 38, Hana, Maui, HI 96713;
(808) 248-8426. 16 units; on the
shore. $–$$

Heavenly Hana Inn
P.O. Box 146, Hana, Maui, HI 96713;
(808) 248-8442. 6 units. $

*"Wriggle while you learn"—hotel hula classes give visitors
a chance to take home a permanent trip memento.*

Restaurants

Adding to mealtime enjoyment, musical entertainment ranges from soothing Hawaiian songs to toe-tapping Tahitian tunes.

This selection is only a sampling of the Valley Isle's restaurants. It's included to give you an idea of the variety of cuisine available throughout the island. You'll make your own discoveries and find some familiar mainland chains. We've included phone numbers when available; it's always wise to make dinner reservations at resort area restaurants.

To help you plan your meal expense, we have added the following guide.

$ Inexpensive
$$ Moderate
$$$ Expensive

Kahului/ Wailuku

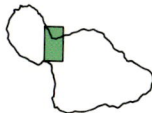

Aloha Restaurant
127 Puunene Ave., Kahului; 877-6318. Unpretentious outside and inside but noted for Hawaiian home-style food; open for lunch and dinner, Sunday brunch. $

Chart House
500 N. Puunene Ave., Kahului; 877-2476. Nice ocean view from this popular seafood, beef, and chicken restaurant; less crowded than Lahaina location. $$

Chum's
1900 Main St., Wailuku. Wide range of cuisine in casual setting; breakfast, lunch and dinner. $

Island Fish House
33 Lono Ave., Kahului; 871-7555. Seafood salon for lunch or dinner; also Kihei sites. $$

Mark Edison's
518 Iao Valley Rd., Wailuku; 242-5555. Unique restaurant in beautiful setting in Iao Needle park. $$

Ming Yuen
162 Alamaha St., Kahului; 871-7787. Industrial area location; good Chinese food; open lunch and dinner. $

Pino's
2065 Main St., Wailuku; 242-9650. Italian food; lunch weekdays, dinner Monday–Saturday. $

Pizza Circus
333 Dairy Rd., Wailuku; 871-1133. Pick up some of the island's best pizza here, try sesame seed-topped crust. $

Red Dragon Chinese Restaurant
Maui Beach Hotel, Kahului; 877-0051. Extensive Chinese buffet nightly (except Monday). $

Sir Wilfred's
Maui Mall, Kahului; 877-3711. Pizza, Tongan bread, soups, and exotic Kona coffee drinks. $

Wailuku Grill
2006 Main St., Wailuku; 244-7505. Good omelets, Belgian waffles, desserts. $

Lahaina/ Kaanapali

Alex's Hole In The Wall
834 Front St., Lahaina; 661-3197. Fresh pasta, seafood, chicken specialties in small Italian restaurant popular with locals; dinner only (closed Sunday). $$

Bettino's
505 Front St., Lahaina; 661-8810. Waterfront window tables, generous portions, mostly Italian; three meals daily. $$

Chart House
1450 Front St., Lahaina; 661-0937. Extremely popular dining spot; no reservations so put your name in early. $$

Chez Paul
820-B Olowalu Village; 661-3843. Small French restaurant, 5 miles south of Lahaina; noted for food, service, wine; dinner only, reservations recommended. $$$

Chopsticks
Royal Lahaina Resort, Kaanapali; 661-3611. All appetizer Asian cuisine; dinner only. $–$$

Discovery Room
Maui Sheraton Hotel, Kaanapali; 661-0031. Breakfast or dine atop Black Rock; dinners include entertainment. $$$

Gerard's
Lahaina Market Place, Lahaina; 661-8939. Nouvelle French cafe, acclaimed sauces and desserts; lunch and dinner. $$$

Greenthums
839 Front St., Lahaina; 667-6126. Perched over the water, casual place for lunch and dinner; bring your own wine. $

Kimo's
845 Front St., Lahaina; 661-4811. Local favorite for seafood and prime rib, try the carrot muffins. $–$$

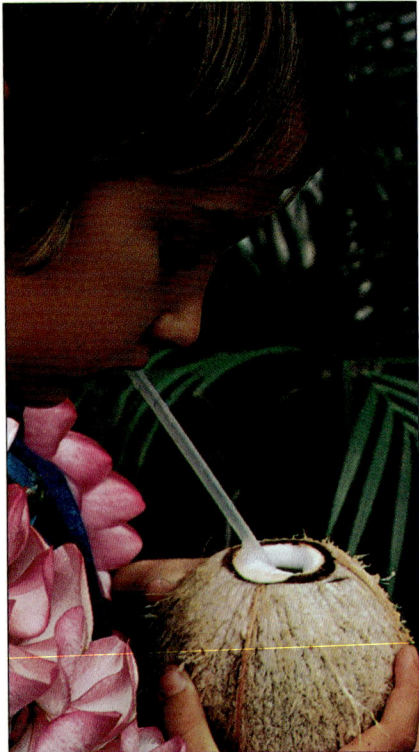

Insert straw and suck, one way to sip coconut milk—straight from the shell.

Tropical treats like these made-on-Maui jams adorn buffet tables around the island.

La Bretagne
562 Front St., Lahaina; 661-8966. French cuisine in old Lahaina house; dinner only. $$

Lahaina Broiler
Front St., Lahaina; 661-3111. City landmark; serves a little bit of everything; breakfast, lunch, and dinner. $–$$

Lahaina Provision Co.
Hyatt Regency Hotel, Kaanapali; 667-7474. Nice location above pool; chocoholic bar; lunch and dinner. $$$

Leilani's
Whalers Village, Kaanapali; 661-4495. Good setting on beach, casual dining; dinner only. $$

Lokelani
Maui Marriott Hotel, Kaanapali; 667-1200. Seafood dining in casual atmosphere, don't miss the after-dinner coffee; reservations suggested. $$$

Longhi's
888 Front St., Lahaina; 667-2288. Visitor and local favorite, greenery-embellished interior, homemade pastas and desserts, fresh seafood; open daily from breakfast. $–$$

Moby Dick's
Royal Lahaina Resort, Kaanapali; 661-3611. Intimate seafood spot; dinner with reservations. $$

Nikko's Steakhouse
Maui Marriott Hotel, Kaanapali Beach; 667-1200. Good Oriental choice for food and showmanship; dinner only. $$

Sam's Beachside Grill
505 Front St., Lahaina; 667-4341. Branch of Sam's in Tiburon, seaside and game specialties; lunch and dinner. $$

Spats II
Hyatt Regency Hotel, Kaanapali; 667-7474. Northern Italian cuisine, intimate atmosphere, one of Maui's hottest nightspots; dinner only, do reserve. $$$

Swan Court
Hyatt Regency Hotel, Kaanapali; 667-7474. Posh decor, stagelike setting with swan-filled lagoon as focus, extensive continental menu, fine wines, impeccable service; reserve for dinner; try macadamia nut pancakes at breakfast brunch. $$$

North of Kaanapali

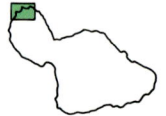

The Bay Club
1 Bay Dr., Kapalua, 669-8008 after 5 P.M., 669-5656 before 5 P.M. Good place for sunset-viewing with pupus and cocktails; romantic gourmet restaurant overlooks sea; lunch and dinner (pianist); well-dressed crowd. $$$

Erik's Seafood Grotto
Kahana Villa (second floor) 4242 Lower Honoapiilani Rd., Kahana; 669-4806. Emphasis on seafood; dinners only (closed Sunday). $$

The Garden
Kapalua Bay Resort Hotel, Kapalua; 669-5656. Tropical plants and Hawaiian open setting adds to dining experience; continental cuisine, fine service; breakfast, grand luncheon buffet, dinner. $$$

Kapalua Grill and Bar
200 Kapalua Dr. (at golf course), Kapalua; 669-5653. Surprisingly pleasant golf course restaurant with wide range of food; lunch and dinner. $$

Market Cafe
Kapalua Bay Hotel Shops, Kapalua; 669-4888. Half of small gourmet market; breakfast, lunch, dinner daily. $

Plantation Veranda
Kapalua Bay Resort, Kapalua; 669-5656. Secluded dinner house, continental cuisine in small formal setting. $$$

Sea House
Napili Kai Beach Club, 5900 Honoapiilani Rd., Napili; 669-6271. Pleasant location, favorite for night-out condo crowd; breakfast, lunch, and dinner; Hawaiian music most nights. $$

Southwest Coast

Azeka's Snack Shop
Azeka Place Shopping Center, S. Kihei Rd., Kihei. Noted for plate lunches; a few picnic tables outdoors. $

Buzz's Wharf
Maalaea Wharf; 244-5426 or 661-0964. Old-time seafood outlet; dinner only. $$

Cafe Kiowai
Maui Prince Hotel, Makena; 874-1111. Open-air cafe with light, new dining; breakfast, lunch, and dinner. $$

Chuck's Steak House
Kihei Town Center, S. Kihei Rd., Kihei; 879-4489. Casual lunch and dinner spot, beef and seafood, nice salad bar; no reservations. $$

Fairway
Wailea Golf Course, Wailea; 879-4060. Outdoor tables, nice views. $$

Hakone
Maui Prince Hotel, Makena; 874-1111. Authentic Japanese cuisine, sushi bar, sukiyaki; dinner. $$

Hong Kong Restaurant
61 S. Kihei Rd., Kihei; 879-2883. Cantonese and Szechwan cuisine; need dinner reservations. $$

Island Fish House
1945 S. Kihei Rd., Kihei; 879-7771. Seafood site, nice wine list; reservations a must. $$

Kiawe Broiler
Maui Inter-Continental Hotel, Wailea; 879-1922. Lunch and informal dinner spot, charcoal-broiled specialties. $$$

Kihei Prime Rib House
2511 S. Kihei Rd., Kihei; 879-1954. Beef, chicken, and seafood dinners in nice setting. $$

Kihei Seas
Rainbow Mall, 2439 S. Kihei Rd., Kihei; 879-5600. Seafood in Polynesian setting, one of Maui's best salad bars; lunch and dinner. $$

Lanai Terrace
Maui Inter-Continental Hotel, Wailea; 879-5600. Sunday brunch setting; make reservations. $$$

La Perouse
Maui Inter-Continental Wailea, Wailea; 879-1922. Award-winning seafood and international specialties in fine setting with background music; Sunday champagne brunch, dinner; reservations a must. $$$

Makena Golf Course Restaurant
161 Makena Rd., Makena; 879-1154. Good course and ocean views while enjoying salads and sandwiches. $–$$

Maui Onion
Stouffer's Wailea Beach Resort, Wailea; 879-4900. Poolside bar, casual lunch spot; try Maui onion rings. $

Palm Court
Stouffer's Wailea Beach Resort, Wailea; 897-4000. International-theme buffet dinners, ocean views; reservations for over 10 people only. $$

Paradise Fruit
1913 S. Kihei Rd., Kihei; Health food snack shop in back of fruit and vegetable market; open 24 hours. $

Prince Court
Maui Prince Hotel, Makena; 874-1111. American cuisine in elegant surroundings, sinful desserts, panoramic views; dinner, Sunday brunch. $$$

Raffles
Stouffer's Wailea Resort, Wailea; 879-4900. Highly praised creative cuisine, fine service; dinner, Sunday brunch. $$$

Sailmaker
Azeka Place Shopping Center, Kihei; 879-4446. Ribs a specialty. $

Wailea Steak House
100 Wailea Ike Dr., Wailea; 879-2875. Popular with locals and visitors, wide selection. $$

Upcountry
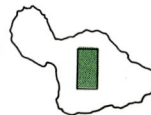

Kula Lodge
Haleakala Hwy., Kula; 878-1535. Dine with a view—both sides of the island; hours vary. $$

Makawao Steak and Fish House
3612 Baldwin Ave., Makawao; 572-8711. Long-time favorite with locals and visitors; salad bar; open from 5 P.M. $$

Mama's Fish House
799 Kaiholo Pl., Paia, Highway 36 1½ miles past Paia; 579-9672. May serve the island's freshest and most creative fish dishes; open for lunch and dinner. $$

Partners
11888 Makawao Ave., Makawao; 572-6611. Casual lunches and dinners feature ribs, steaks, chicken, and pizza. $

Picnics
Paia; 579-8021. Popular local place; packs picnic lunches for Hana travelers.

Polli's
1202 Makawao Ave., Makawao; 572-7808. Small Mexican restaurant with vegetarian specialties (also in Kihei); lunch Tuesday–Saturday, daily dinner, Sunday brunch. $

Pukalani Terrace Country Club
360 Pukalani Rd., Pukalani; 572-1325. Off the 18th green with good West Maui views; lunch, dinner, and Sunday brunch. $

Hana
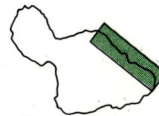

Hana Ranch Restaurant
Hana; 248-8211. One of the few places to eat in East Maui; breakfast and lunch, dinner on weekends. $

Hotel Hana Maui
Hana; 248-8211. Haven for road-weary travelers; garden surroundings; coffee shop, poolside dining, luncheon buffet in main dining room; evening dining with Hawaiian entertainment, reservations required. $–$$$

Index